Equity in American Education

To order additional copies, please contact us.
BookSurge, LLC
www.booksurge.com
1-866-308-6235
orders@booksurge.com

J. BRUCE BURKE and
MICHELLE JOHNSTON

EQUITY IN AMERICAN EDUCATION

2006

Equity in American Education

TABLE OF CONTENTS

PREFACE

The twenty-first century brings another millennium in which American Education still searches to provide equity for all students; and issues of justice and compassion in our schools are yet to be addressed adequately. Access to a college education is so elusive that nearly a third of American youth are excluded from participation. The costs, admission standards, and academic fortitude required to attend post secondary education are prohibitive for many and decisions are often made on political and economic grounds rather than educational standards.

The authors have been teacher educators, in Michigan, throughout our careers; we have contributed to reform and improvements in schools and universities, but find our efforts nearly overwhelmed by the circumstances of our culture, economy, and social organizations. Jennifer Gransholm, Governor of Michigan, wants every child in her state to complete a college education; yet the State of Michigan, which ranks 50th economically in the United States cannot afford to educate every child through college, although it has the infrastructure to do so. State aid to the post-secondary institutions ranges from around 20% to less than 40% of actual costs. Colleges and universities still have to find ways to pay for more professors and larger infrastructure to teach all of those students who Governor Grandholm wants taught. The situation is especially sad because Michigan needs a high-tech work force to move forward economically and culturally. But, the state is frustrated in this ambition, leaving a huge portion of its children and youth in rural and urban locations uneducated and unprepared for the twenty-first century. This book asks: how do we fulfill the dream of having all children to succeed educationally through college graduation. This is an especially challenging dream when so many children, particularly minority children, experience schools on the margins of mainstream academia?

We believe that education is a community affair and is carried on in arenas of communication. Talking, reading, writing, responding to the circumstances of school and classroom are the substances of teaching. "The teacher is a special kind of reader; one embedded in making sense of texts and being a moral text to students (Burke, 1999)." This book seeks to make sense of the current scene in schools and communities and provoke serious discussions about where education and access to it is going in America.

We wish to thank various colleagues and friends who have contributed to our understanding of schools, curricula, and teaching. Namely, our special thanks go to Gerry Duffy, Dick Allington, Cleo Cherryholmes, Susan Melnick, and David Labaree. We also thank Dean Carole Ames for her support for continuing research, study and writing, while assigned administrative responsibilities as well as teaching in the College of Education at Michigan State University. Thanks, also, go to Michael Harris, Vice President of Academic Affairs at Ferris State University.

Several of the chapters in this book have appeared in other publications or formats over the last few years. Chapter One was published in a special issue of the *Journal of Race, Class, and Gender: Part III,* Fall, 2004, Vol. 11, #3, 19-35. Chapter Two was published substantially in the current form in *Higher Education in Europe*, Vol. XXIX, No. 1, April, 2004. And Chapter Eight was presented as a paper at the *International Conference on Social Science*, November 11-13, 2004 in New Orleans, LA. At the beginning of each chapter one may find quotations form poems we wrote and published in *The Tao of Teaching, A Poetic Interpretation*. Paris, France: Sophia Press, 1999. We dedicate the book to our spouses: Susan Burke and Tom Johnston. Without their support and discussions, the work would not have been finished.

"If you are going to teach,
Learn the way of moderation.
Moderation starts with submission.
Submission lets virtue grow
Without making it a competition..."
No. 59, *The Tao of Teaching*

CHAPTER ONE
Students at the Margins

When Joseph Aguerrebere (2003) shares his personal story of being a first-generation, college student from East Los Angeles, he describes making decisions about college according to the color of the football uniforms, proximity to his home, and financial aid, with no consideration regarding the quality of the programs or his place in the milieu. He also relates his experiences as a first-generation, post-secondary student from urban high school where he had no one to guide or prepare him for his encounters in college like many students from similar backgrounds and environments. For example, during his first college-level test, when the instructor told him to fill a "blue book," a common examination booklet used in colleges, he did not know what to do or what to write. His narrative is similar to others for whom going to college is an elusive part of the American dream; a dream, which in the past, eluded them and their family members because of gender, race, ethnicity, class, income, or geographic location, specifically being raised in extreme urban and rural regions.

Everyone should have a chance, so the dream goes, to go to college, get a degree, find a job, enter the mainstream of America's economic success story, and emerge from their cocoons to experience the empowerment of the larger society. For many, however, this dream turns into a nightmare from which they emerge in debt with feelings of inadequacy and defeat. Many students cannot repay the debt on their college loans because they cannot get jobs. The nightmare and feelings of defeat experienced in college exacerbate their concepts of low self-esteem and strengthen their sense of victimhood that formed in their early years of schooling. Unfortunately, many students join their peers and become members of the approximately 30 percent of those students who get accepted to a college or university and fail to graduate. Many fail in the first year of study, particularly first-generation students. This statistic is problematical because Americans link a college education with success so thoroughly that anything short of a college degree seems like failure. Setting aside the question of whether everybody can or should go to college, most Americans believe that not succeeding in college leads to economic and social failure. Specifically, the Bureau of Labor Statistics (www.bls.gov), which documents, compiles, and reports wage trends, shows data that suggest years of education, particularly the acquisition of a baccalaureate degree, contribute to the improvement of personal earning power.

Marginalization and Society.

The college failure rate might be more acceptable if it were distributed evenly across all groups in our society. The truth of the matter, however, is that a marginal group of youth accounts for the highest percentage of failure (McWhorter, 2000, pp. 85-89), as compared to their advantaged peers who graduate. By marginal group, we mean a collection of young citizens who experience "marginalization" by high schools and colleges in the United States, and who the human community devalues (Kegan, 1994, p.341). Essentially, race, gender, class, and immigration status stigmatize those who make up this marginal population. They come from diverse racial groups, including African-Americans, Hispanic-Americans, and Native-Americans. They are also female and poor, whether they come from the urban centers or from the rural periphery of the American population. Many of these students experience marginalization through the expectations held by their schools, communities, families, peers, and selves. When we interviewed a principal from a poor, isolated rural community about the relatively low achievement of her students during their high school years, she said that it was "good enough." The question is: For whom is the low achievement good enough?

These marginalized students, whose achievement is "good enough" for some, experience difficulty in reading and writing English fluently, they have limited mathematics skills, and many are computer illiterate as well as technologically unprepared. Almost all of them possess little academic fortitude; academic fortitude, defined as the ability to negotiate the rigors of college study, including how to manage time, study, and interact with professors. Let's make this point clear: there is nothing wrong with these students as human beings; they are not "marginal human beings." Instead, we use the term "marginal" to describe the *treatment* these students receive as a group that has handicapped them as scholars. The higher education standards setters view these students as handicapped because they lack crucial academic skills, which include being self-directed learners (Kegan, 1994, p.281) who can navigate academe and, as a result, they enter post-secondary education being treated as failures. Without academic success, chances are that they will continue life on the margins where other opportunities for personal growth will continue to escape them. In the end, the unstated implication is that such youth are less valuable human beings than the rest of the "academically successful" population.

How did this situation evolve? How did it happen that race, gender, income, and class became barriers to success in higher education, the so-called bastion of liberal ideals in America, as Diane Ravitch suggested in *Left Back: A Century of Failed School Reforms (2000)?* Is the answer that students who exist on the margins are miss-educated? Consider the idea that human abilities are evenly distributed across all ethnic and racial groups, a position for which there is considerable evidence (see: Seligman, D., 1992; Harris, 1998), then one has to ask why the marginalized students in the United States education system are predominantly African-Americans, Hispanic-Americans, urban youth, Native-Americans, rural poor, and migrant workers' children. These sub-groups make up the majority of the marginal students failing in universities; they have lower incomes, poverty, and lower welfare assistance when compared with whites (Williams, 2003, p. 359). They also have in common families who have not participated in the American dream of economic and social success, as well as coming from unsafe and restrictive environments. Some seek the post-secondary environment as a safe haven from the gangs of the street and strife of the family. The problem is so blatant that poverty, racism, and class issues seem to define American education for marginal students.

Interestingly, when Dr. Martin Luther King spoke in Riverside Church in New York City, about Vietnam in 1967, he identified the miseducated youth on the margins as those serving in the military. At that time, he asked for changes in education and society because he feared that the poor urban and rural youth, like those serving in the military in 1967, would continue to be marginalized. Dr. King was correct, because almost 40 years later the marginalization persists and in more insidious ways that prevent the poor as well as racially and ethnically diverse students from succeeding. Thernstrom & Thernstrom (2003) demonstrate that segregation has not been reduced in the four decades since Dr. King's speech. They point out that over 70 percent of all African-American students attend a minority school, that is, they go to schools where they are the dominate majority (p. 175). Gary Orfield writes about what he calls an "Index of Exposure," which refers to the exposure of minority students to white students. He and his colleagues conclude that the minority students are "segregated" because the white students are so few in number in their schools. This reality reinforces a commonly held minority view that they are "different" from whites, making them, they believe, less capable of learning at the college level.

Why is it that the lack of academic success is experienced by students and their families as personal inadequacy? One answer is that blaming the victim has a long history in America and is rooted in the individualistic understanding of society. Elaine Brown (2003) discusses blame when she points to the marked differences in college attendance between whites and non-whites and the poor. She hypothesizes that society is quick to demonize and blame the marginalized because they are different than the majority or middle class. From the beginnings of American democracy, puritan ideals of individual success have defined good and evil. Andrew Carnegie's *Gospel of Wealth* openly preached the message that wealth was evidence of goodness. The celebration of individualism in America cuts deeply into our self-evaluations. All success is credited to individual striving, so too, it follows that failure must be due to individual inadequacy of some kind. Those who struggle and fail are open to self-loathing; they suspect that society is right in judging them to be flawed and to blame them for the flaw whether or not that flaw is based on such uncontrollable traits as race, ethnicity, or gender.

This cultural ethos impacts the classroom environments and requirements of the students beginning post-secondary, gatekeeper classes, such as freshmen English. The gatekeeper environments and their accompanying instructional practices reinforce the negative, unproductive, self-defeating feeling of the marginalized students. Such classes implicitly teach these students to think, "If I am failing English, I must truly be dumb. I should flunk and leave college." So, those educators who seek to make a difference in the lives of marginal students must take on the challenge to rid our programs of such invidious self-deprecations. Nonetheless, the challenge is a deep and mighty obstacle. In the Great Depression, when nearly a third of all Americans were out of work through no fault of their own, the common assumption among the victims of unemployment was that something was wrong with them (Kennedy, 1999, p. 174).

Donaldo Macedo (1994) strongly contends that "institutions, particularly schools, reproduce the dominant ideology through a web of lies that distort and transfigure reality (p. 37)." He views this as happening through an "over-celebration of myths that...degrade and devalue other cultural narratives along the lines of race, ethnicity, language, and gender (p. 37)." Further, he contends that approaches to literacy improvement, such as "competency-based" literacy programs (p. 35) are so often earmarked for the poor and underachieving students and actually have the consequences of undermining future academic success for these students. So, the very vehicle designed to solve a problem in literacy ends up perpetuating the problem, leading the marginalized students to be more disenfranchised and less likely to succeed in a post-secondary environment.

An urban-minority student, who struggled with freshman English, reported that he enjoyed English in college, but it was harder than high-school English because the books were different and he was not used to them. After being probed about the differences in the books, he said that in high school the books did not require answering questions in class, discussing the stories, and writing about them. His perception of differences in the books was not correct; the difference was in pedagogy. The contrast is between the pedagogy of academic engagement and discourse versus the pedagogy of miseducating the under-prepared. Because he had not engaged in discourse in his high school English classes, he felt inadequate in college.

Views of the Ivory Tower: Luck and Work

The traditional view holds that all college students are privileged. Those who enter and succeed should think of themselves as lucky, not virtuous. After all, everyone has seen *Animal House* and similar movies depicting the fun-filled halcyon days of college life. An uncle summarized this view by defining "College Bred" as four years of "loaf." In fact, college students must come to terms with their very good luck and recognize that their time in college also requires appropriate preparation and serious industry. Likewise, those who hold the keys of the gates to college success must remember that someone else opened those very gates for them, but not all are as lucky. Students on the margins often have financial and family burdens that remove them from the mainstream of college life and make every moment a struggle to survive. Maureen, for instance, is a single mother in her mid-twenties whose work and financial aid barely kept her tuition, shelter, food, and daycare expenses met. Maureen can study and meet her academic obligations only after she solves the other problems of her day-to-day survival. There is another young woman with whom we worked who was raised by an ailing grandmother and found out that she had to care for her younger siblings during the second semester of her first year in college because her grandmother had a stroke. She had to abandon her goals for a degree to become a responsible guardian to her siblings. These tales are not uncommon and not tales of personal failure, but stories of young people on the margins unable to attain their dreams.

In her popular novel about class and family strife in a North Carolina community, Deborah Smith, *The Stone Flower Garden*, (2002) writes about an exchange between the village matriarch, a prepubescent mathematical genius, and his father. The matriarch tells the father and mathematical genius that she can offer the son a college scholarship that will change the course of the family. Seeing the father's stunned reaction, the matriarch tells him that it is worth the sacrifice. Although Smith's writing is fiction, her message rings true. Going to college can change the course of a family, and it does require sacrifice. However, for some, the sacrifice is alienation from the family and culture with little to show in terms of success.

Crediting college failure to individual inadequacies is an invidious strategy to perpetuate racial, gender, and class segregation by inviting marginal students to embrace blame and look askance at the difference effort makes in achievement. In addition to social blame, the individual student often feels torn between academic success and identification with a group. The tension between academic success and failure is also a cultural conflict. Professors confirm observations of this cultural conflict when students struggle with differences in religion, lifestyle, affluence, and questioning strategies, which, for the marginalized, often means answering yes or no rather than engaging in a debate. Further, some black children will choose academic failure so as not to be identified with white, successful kids (Scholfield, 1981).

While America values individual competitiveness, there remains a deep suspicion of the value of education itself, other than as a credentialing function. Working-class families experience education as a source of dislocation (Dews and Law, 1995). Education is seen as an opportunity, but it also creates a cultural gap between student and family/community, whether the community is an isolated rural community, a Native-American reservation, or an ethnic urban neighborhood. The sense of disloyalty some working-class students experience as they engage in higher education makes them feel uncomfortable in both settings: with the family and on the campus. A spiritual gap widens as students feel more and more alienated from family, friends and town. They learn a new language of discourse: "You talk funny since you went to college." Stay-at-home friends claim they do not know these college students anymore and gradually the gap widens (Kegan, 1994; Kegan and Lakey, 2001). People, like organizations, want to grow and improve; however, as Kegan and Lakey (2001) remind us, there are competing commitments. Also, there is the "new second-generation" phenomenon discussed by Portes and Rumbaut (2001), which describes how naive immigrant parents are compared with their American-born children who have had to face the bitter realities of American schools.

Reality of College Life

College students currently have less financial support from their families than previous generations of students in a period of time when college costs are escalating. They find they have to work marginal jobs to make ends meet and still they have to borrow money to pay tuition. For those students at the margins, the financial obligations for college are at crisis levels. One puzzled professor who sought reasons for his students attending class exhausted and unprepared learned that they had to work cleaning up Chili's or Applebee's or other similar establishments until after the 2 A.M. closing times. The students who work away from the campus and its activities feel left out of college life, as does Maureen who is raising a child, working, and completing her baccalaureate degree. They do worse academically than others who can devote more time to their studies. Kegan (1994) also reminds us that the content of much of the college curriculum of post-modernism seem to be the irrelevant privilege or confusing and even demeaning to marginalized students and their families.

In addition to experiencing college as a different culture, marginalized students feel a sense of futility, fear of failure, and anger at the "system" (McWhorter, 2003, p. 154). They feel the bind of either not being good enough, and tend to blame themselves, or they deliberately aim for lower grades because they may think getting good grades is a "white thing." Marginal students experience a duality of damnation: first, they experience the discouragement of high-stakes competition in college and the fear that they will fail, and second, they experience the cultural/spiritual gap between campus and home and the accompanying fear of success. So, both options look bleak. "If I fail to succeed in college, I bring shame on myself and my family; and if I succeed in college, I become some other kind of person no one at home knows." This damned-if-I-do and damned-if-I-don't double-mindedness is so strong for some students that it may account for their dropping out in anger, just to get rid of it. One first-year student-athlete from a tiny rural community reported to his dean that he could not fail because his "dad was in the trades and wanted (him) to have a better life." How could he have a better life if he failed in college? Yet, how could he succeed if it meant rejecting his father and his trade? He had feelings of inadequacy because his high school apparently did not prepare him for college English. For example, he had trouble answering "open-ended" questions which require him to think through an idea, not just name a fact. This concern leads us to ask: Why do the marginalized students have educational experiences that appear to be more literal, rather than critical? Without engagement in symbolic discourse, students are not truly prepared for participating in the culture of academe.

High schools urge their students to go to college. Students continuing their education beyond high school are a mark of good schools, or so it is thought. The 57 percent of high-school students who do continue their education by going to post-secondary institutions includes a wide diversity of students and their qualifications for advanced studies. Some public colleges and universities recruit minority and working-class students to match the demographic proportions of the state. They are successful in this effort. Take California as an example; with 54 percent of all high-school students are minority students and post-secondary institutions enroll 53 percent minorities. The problem with these minority enrollments is that many are not adequately prepared to meet the rigors of college academic life and the colleges are not prepared to offer remedial assistance to the students they recruit. For example, some urban students entering college have a limited mathematics background. This is often due to program unavailability and a paucity of materials and assistance easily available to their suburban counterparts. We have found an increasing national sentiment against remediation programs as being too expensive and too difficult to help students who have been neglected academically for a dozen years. Yet, colleges knowingly admit students who will have a very difficult time succeeding in the current college climate.

A history professor who teaches at a Michigan university voiced his outrage at the university strategy of taking money from minority students by admitting them and then eventually failing them out of school. "I feel like I am participating in a vast criminal conspiracy...we take their money and take their dignity," he is quoted as saying. (Reported in the *Detroit News;* July 15, 2001). Many universities have special programs to help marginal students but they have a poor success rate. Graduation rates for African-Americans have not improved over the last decade, in spite of remediation efforts. Nationally, only about 40 percent of blacks enrolled will graduate from college, compared with 60 percent of whites enrolled. Urban black students who go to the large public universities find themselves in large classes, surrounded by whites and Asians and feel isolated and intimidated, not understanding the culture and its language of academe (Kegan, 1994, 2001). For marginal students, overcoming the barriers of academic standards is only part of the picture. They must also overcome the barriers of social, cultural, and economic class on campus especially in the introductory course classrooms where students first encounter the discourse of academe. Professors expect students to be prepared and are little interested in explaining the niceties of plagiarism standards and proper references for writing essays. Plagiarism is so common in freshmen English courses that one can suspect it is a major instrument for weeding out "unqualified" or ill-prepared students.

We followed thirty marginal students across a fall semester at Ferris State University (FSU). Of the thirty students, only nine survived the semester. The marginal students could not decode the protocols of college life and academic instructions. For example, one student got sick and was granted a temporary medical leave to go home. The student stayed home the entire semester and was surprised to find that her professors recorded failing grades for all her courses for failure to attend. She thought medical leave excused her from these course demands. She felt she was a victim of an institutional "gotcha game." Her story is not uncommon. When sharing our findings with faculty working with first-year students in other universities, they reported students being absent for weeks and months to care for family matters, because their families expected their attendance at times of family crises. These students often feel pulled by the family to maintain traditions that are counterproductive in academe.

Reducing the margins
Irvin Peckham writes (Dews and Law, 1995, p.263) about

what he calls "The Complicity of Codes: The Exclusionary Function of Educational Institutions," in which he says colleges, "reproduce the existing social structure by screening out students from the working-class and consequently reserving for the children of the professional and managerial classes the privileges that attend academic success." Professor Peckham sees the norms of university codes as written by professionals who have a class bias favoring the professional and manager class versus the working class. Therefore, Peckham would explain the race for academic success as "fixed" in favor of the professional class (p. 275). There is some truth to Peckham's judgment that the playing field of university life is uneven, or that the race is fixed. Nonetheless, we do not accept this judgment as the final word. That which is uneven can be made plain; the fixed can be unfixed. Marginalization need not be the response of academic institutions to those of racial, ethnic, gender and class differences. Remediation can work, even if it has not worked well in the past. The keys to making an even playing field are: 1) starting early in students' academic path to prepare them for post secondary education; and 2) transform the experience and expectations of college faculty to teach by reaching out to their students.

The Head Start program gives us a clue. If we were to keep up such good beginnings, such as the Head Start program provides throughout the public school years and into community college and public universities, a difference could be achieved. Of course, what we recommend will been seen as another layer of reform on educational systems in America. Perhaps the key is also to create communities of academic development that start early; at least in the middle-school years. How many of us have had someone, some teacher, some administrator or counselor make a difference in our lives, by taking an interest in our success? One marginal student at FSU told his professor that he did not think about attending college, or even consider it until a teacher took an interest in him. The teacher gave him an application blank and financial aid forms for FSU; then he sat down and helped the student complete the forms. This student remains a successful graduate student in the FSU School of Criminal Justice today because someone invested time with him and provided the concrete help he needed at that point in his life. We propose to make such initiatives more formal, more structured, and offered earlier in the public school career of marginal students. The university and the public schools should be recruiting the potential college-bound from among the different racial, gender, and class populations that exist in a state.

Instead of seeing a growing outreach to minority students, we find neglect. The youth existing at the margins and the victims of inadequate educations are, according to Bob Herbert (2001, September 3), "dangerously disconnected from the nation's social and economic mainstream." They are becoming members of the growing legions of the unemployed and unemployable. Not only do they have limited work or employability skills, the youth at the margins have limited literacy, numeracy, and other skills associated with academic success and fortitude.

A college student (identified by Herbert as Tony) who failed academically, went home after his first year of college to find that there were no jobs for him in his urban community where unemployment is rampant. The realization that he was "nowhere" was an epiphany for Tony, who reenrolled in college with renewed commitment and vigor. Returning to college was difficult for Tony who was faced with financial stumbling blocks. He also lacked the background knowledge necessary to adequately read the volumes of assignments, write understandably, and compute—all skills that were neglected in his elementary and secondary schooling. Although Tony has some college experience, he is as unemployable as a high school drop-out.

Tony is not the only student in this margin of nowhere. According to the findings of a study by the Center for Labor and Market at Northeastern University (Boston), 54 out of every 100 people looking for a job do not have high school diplomas. Herbert (2001, September 3) reports that one quarter of the high school graduates are unemployed. The study on which Herbert relies was published in 1999 when the economy was good. What are the prospects of employment for America's undereducated youth during the current economic downturn?

Furthermore, we err when we view the disconnected youth as young men. According to Herbert, when he reported the Northeastern University study, many are young women, without work and school, and who run the increased risks of pregnancy. The cycle then continues with young women on the margins raising children alone, and in poverty, thus placing another generation at risk and in the margins, unable to read, compute, and engage in the activities of the mainstream.

Learning from other cultures

In China, where literacy is a major value and therefore, a curriculum issue, school policymakers and administrators continually quote the mantra that an illiterate mother means an illiterate child. China provides the schools with the means to teach literacy to all children and their parents where necessary. In America, likewise, children born on the margins where access to literacy is a problem will continue to be lives of illiteracy, limited hope, diminished expectations, and poor educations that perpetuate victimization. America has too many mothers with low literacy skills and limited academic understanding to be models and guides for their children on the pathway to achievement and success. We conclude that a solution to public literacy would require higher education institutions joining with public education in providing the resources for recruiting students and engaging them with the challenges of academic fortitude.

We were on a trip to China last year accompanying a group of teachers from the Midwest who were visiting schools and colleges in China as a cultural tour and exchange. One incident stood out for us. One of the American teachers asked a Chinese teacher what they did with students who couldn't read. "How do you teach them?" she asked. The Chinese teacher answered: "This is not a problem for us, because everybody reads. If a child cannot read, we teach that child to read, so there are none who are left out." Most of the American teachers did not really believe this answer. They thought the Chinese were covering up their failures in the classroom by making what for them was a "policy statement."

What is missing in the American teachers' professional repertoire is a healthy dose of optimism. A teacher must believe that his or her students can learn and learn successfully, even in the face of all kinds of evidence to the contrary. This optimism is the first criterion because unless a teacher believes in the students' capacities for success, nothing else is possible. Students know immediately when their teacher looks down on them, distrusts them, and is cynical about their chances for success. Disrespecting students is a way out of the responsibility of teaching students, and through disrespect, we disinvite students to succeed in an academic environment

(Purkey and Novak, 1996). Marginalized students don't receive the academy's invitation to succeed.

Teaching for success and changing the structures for success

To teach is to communicate the substance, meaning, and love of the subjects being taught. But what many teachers expect is that students come to class with the love of learning already embedded in them. If that is the situation, what is left for the teacher to do but offer approval for what the students have already learned? Consequently, those students who have not already acquired the subject, skills, or knowledge receive disapproval.

There is always tension between nature and nurture. Teachers must be committed to the nurture side of the tension. There remains a long-standing resistance on the part of teachers for taking responsibility for students' nurturing. Thirty years ago, in Lansing, Michigan, the school district was under a court order to desegregate by busing. This meant that students were shifted by ethnicity to produce a greater balance among students of color in the city's schools. The effect was particularly noted by the high-school teachers. In one of the high schools where there was a traditional reputation for high academic standards, the teachers came forward to complain about the impact of busing on their school. They said the students were not prepared to read English literature and to study algebra and geometry. As a result, the teachers said they could not teach these students. At the time we listened to their complaints and told them that what they seemed to want were students who do not need their teaching. We said, "You want students who already know how to read Shakespeare or do algebra." They countered by insisting that they were unable to do anything with unprepared and unmotivated students. Many of these teachers retired from teaching at the end of that first year of school busing.

There has been a paradigm change since those Michigan teachers were prepared to teach. No longer are ideas considered as "out there," and waiting to be discovered. Rather, ideas are understood as tools—like forks and knives and microchips—that people devise to cope with the world in which they find themselves. Gerald Graff (2003) puts it this way: "Academic intellectual culture is a conversation, rather than a mere inventory of texts, facts, ideas, and methods (p. 27). Those Michigan teachers really did not want to teach their students. They thought that students should come to their classes already smart, self-disciplined, and not a bother to their teachers. These teachers conceived their role as a critic of their students and they used the power of their grade book to keep students in line. In other words, these teachers thought: "I am in charge and you (students) must do what I say to do, must think what I want you to think, and believe in teachers' authority." Such teachers believe that they are in command of their classrooms. However, when teachers ignore the "power of their students' ideas" (Deborah Meier) and hand down their ideas from "on high," they teach a simplistic vision of ideas and their usefulness. The temptation is to simplify all questions as having answers that are either right or wrong, and all moral issues as either good or bad. Louis Menand in his fine book, *The Metaphysical Club* (2001), reminds us rightly that American pragmatism believes that ideas should never become ideologies.

Access to higher education transcends economic assistance and racial blind admissions policies and includes genuine academic fortitude. That is, students must gain access to the academic culture of higher education. Howard Gardner (1999) points out how difficult it is for even the best students from the best schools to make the transition to university curricular culture. "Despite years of schooling, the minds of these college students remain fundamentally unschooled. (p. 120)." So, it should be no surprise that many of the economically marginal students who manage to gain admission to college fail in their first year and drop out of school. The causes of failure are many, but in our experience two major issues tend to dominate: 1) the lack of a genuine preparation of marginal students for college academic life; and 2) the lack of a nurturing academic culture once admitted that is supportive of marginal students. The solution to offering students genuine access to higher education, therefore, goes beyond providing material means for financial access.

If new college students are not prepared for the rigors of college academic life, one view suggests that they emerged from their secondary schools as undereducated without true understanding of the meaning of success. Further, if high school seniors want to go to college, but cannot be accepted because of low grades, low-test scores, or a perceived unavailability of scholarships, are they not wasting time in secondary school? If a college student is charged with plagiarism and suspended, was he or she simply wasting time in secondary school? If a high school senior does not know how to use a computer and draws upon the resources of the internet and local libraries via on-line networks, was not time in secondary school wasted? If a student has been wasting time in school and the school or school district has done nothing about it in 12 years, why is the student blamed for the waste? We know that learning is a contextual phenomenon, socially constructed and culturally administered, so why are individuals blamed for personal failure? If a student does not know how to read at the time of entering secondary school, was he or she at fault after six to eight years in a public school that teaches reading as its basic responsibility?

The shame of American education is the institutional failure to teach reading and basic mathematics to the school-age population. The double shame is that the majority of non-readers are racial minorities and from the lower economic class. Millions of American do not read and cannot function in a literate-intensive environment. When remediation is offered to non-readers, marginally literate instructors often staff the courses.

What we are exploring at FSU and other sister institutions in Michigan is the construction of special organizational relationships among secondary schools, community colleges, and universities with the goal of championing the education of marginal students. We need to cut through the organizational morass that confines students to four years of high school and then four years of college. We want to identify those students who, with special assistance, can cut through high school and two years of community college in approximately four years. At the same time, these students must be able to read, write, compute, and use technology prior to entering a university-level academic major. We also must communicate high expectations for success in school and life after school. These students need to know that D- does not mean passing and that life requires performing at an A+ effort.

A major part of the problem is institutional obsession with "what students know" in content knowledge, rather than identification of "what students can do," as in process knowledge. The *New York Times* reported in 2001 about a special program for talented kids in New York City who were allowed to take college-level courses in their junior year of high school. City University of New York (CUNY) was going to accept these students at third-year university status after they had successfully completed two years in the program. We say that if given concentrated, focused, expert help, any student could do this and avoid wasting time sitting out high school. Wasting time is the most costly process in schools. We could pay for such a program by having the state-based secondary school allocation for each student recruited to the program set aside to support the costs. If we focused on early advanced help, we could eliminate the cost of remedial studies at the university level, as students would enter the university in their 19th year with two years of traditional college credit work completed. In European universities a 19-year-old student is considered a mature university student with languages, basic mathematics, and social studies completed. They become responsible for themselves and attend lectures, tutorials, and laboratories until they are ready to take exams and "graduate."

If we are to succeed in such a project, we will have to reach out to the marginal populations in our schools, way in advance of college level course participation. Instead of having unprepared students in college, we should assure that students are advanced enough to participate fully in the academic life. We have been teaching, currently, a one-hour per week orientation class to college freshmen as an experiment. The class has twenty students who we follow closely in their academic struggles: four are inner-city students, a few are suburbanites, and the rest are from rural settings. The students from the rural backgrounds are stunned by the size of the college; the suburban students act like little smarties with no goals and are full of prejudices of several stripes; and the inner-city students are not easily classified as being of a single type. Joe, for example, mostly sleeps through class and only seems engaged when he's telling stories about his life, like the time he bought two buckets of chicken wings and some bottles of whiskey. He reports that he drove around Detroit eating and drinking and throwing the chicken bones out of the car windows. Two of the young female students recognized that they needed academic help, particularly for reading for deep meaning and answering critical questions. Sam, the gang member, wears his do rag and jail pants and checks his cell phone repeatedly. Several of the rural students tell stories about their drunken parents and the dangers of home life. To inspire them, we ask them to write something in every class, including biographical reflections. We also ask them to send weekly emails to the instructor describing their goals, strengths, weaknesses and frustrations.

What we are learning about marginal students in higher education and their needs is matched by what we know about the prejudices of university professors about secondary school and community college instructors. University personnel, at most institutions, tend to believe they are superior workers over the "lower level" workers. They, after all, participated in years of education and professional inquiry. The disregard of community college's positive role in higher education is really a form of sexism, class bias, and racism, rather than a judgment on the quality of academic work performed in community colleges.

Some universities offer advisor training to uncover hidden biases, prejudices, and assumptions in dealing with diverse students. Michigan State University operates an Office of

Racial Ethnic Student Affairs, which provides university-wide training programs to improve the staff perceptions of diverse students. In such training sessions, both self-awareness and communication and advising skills are addressed. They argue that behavioral change often precedes attitudinal change, so they work on adjusting advisors' behaviors in spite of the assumptions, biases, and prejudices advisors may carry.

While individual change is a worthy final goal, it is often extremely difficult to achieve without structural and organizational change. We are not going to make the world of higher education a better place for marginalized students by converting individuals to "right beliefs" and "right behaviors" one person at a time. Only when higher education organizations change will improvements on the part of the individual emerge. For example, a director of vocational certification reports that 32 to 45 percent of the students in vocational/career centers are labeled as some type of special-need student; i.e., they are learning-disabled, emotionally impaired, etc., and/or participating in alternative education programs. Almost all of these students are poor, but the labels exclude them from high-stakes testing and again, they are disinvited to succeed in education (Purkey and Novak, 1996). By removing these students from the testing cycle and placing them in vocational centers, the local school averages look better. The administrators look good for deciding to provide individual assistance, through vocational education programs and, as a result of such assistance have the students out of the testing pool for the school district.

In vocational/career centers over time, the students are almost certain to drop dramatically in their reading, writing, and mathematics skills. They are trained for entry-level job skills, such as small engine repair and continue to remain at the job entry level, while the more technical jobs are shipped overseas. Pushing non-performing, low literacy students into vocational/career tech centers sounds like the old days when the special-education students were put in school basements. They are out of sight and out of the mainstream system. What happens to these students when they get the entry-level jobs that are available? They remain at the level of non-achievement, blame others for their situation, get frustrated, and support causes that place blame, and do not support the basic tenets of democracy, which could improve their lives. Deep in American class-consciousness is the belief that racial differences account for educational differences. It does not matter, it seems, that researchers have time and again debunked the belief in intelligence or educational capacity as rooted in racial identity (Harris, 1998, p. 251). Still, the expectations hold fast: "blacks cannot compete with whites in higher education;" "females cannot compete with males in mathematics;" and "the poor are less competitive than the rich." By holding fast to these beliefs and implementing systems that perpetuate them, educational systems actually provide the means for executing results that confirm their beliefs.

Higher education can, however, work for everybody. But it may not be the same "higher education" for everybody. A major example may explain this principle. There is an ongoing effort to recruit, educate and support new teachers for Native-American schools in Michigan. The need for Native-American teachers is high; for example, even in the tribal K-12 schools such as Nah Tah Wash and Bahweting Anishable there are only one or two Native-American teachers. At the Bay Mills Community College, a tribal college in the northern peninsula,

55 percent of the students are Indian, but there are only two Native-American instructors. An agreement has been achieved between the Bay Mills Community College and FSU to recruit students to a Native-American Teacher Education program in which the first half of the program will take place in Bay Mills and the second half in FSU in Big Rapids (Lower Peninsula). Non-Native-American teachers seldom understand the cultural and political issues underlying curriculum and instruction. For the most part, Native-American students have not been well served by the current educational paradigms. The under-representation of teachers from other minority groups creates cultural and political conflict in classrooms that are becoming transformed demographically as minority groups edge toward majority domination in schools. The agreement to prepare Native-American teachers for Native-American schools was a significant one; but it was quickly found to be a difficult challenge to achieve. Up to 50% of Native-Americans students leave secondary school before graduation; only 17% of those who do graduate from high school, go on to some form of post-secondary higher education (Goggins, Williams & Radin, 1997). Only a very small percentage of that number in higher education is pursuing teacher education; and only a few who become certified teachers stay in the teaching profession beyond three years (Thomason, 1999).

So, what must be done is the identification of promising Native-American students earlier in the public school cycle, no later than middle school level for example. These students must be recruited, given special attention in reading, writing, mathematics, and computer literacy. Since the issue to be faced in such a project includes race (North American natives), class (poverty levels of the families), and gender (preference for boys over girls), all three issues must be addressed early on in the recruiting and foundation process. If students and their families are to buy into the project, they must experience positive orientation to a culturally sensitive curriculum and a poverty alleviation road path over the secondary school years.

Because most Native-Americans live in poor rural areas, they experience many forms of isolation that impede their academic achievement. They experience "community isolation" in not having access to information and opportunities due to cultural disparities between the students' community and the society as a whole. They experience "educational isolation" in not having access to innovations and advanced level courses, such as algebra and geometry, not to mention calculus. They experience "vocational isolation" in not having access to mentors, training, and work opportunities, such as seasonal employment. And finally, they experience "family isolation" in not having access to schooling through family and cultural disenfranchisement because many Native-American parents do not participate in support of local schools.

Beginning early, students recruited to such a program would be connected by their personal laptop computers. They would have designated mentors in critical areas of academic development, such as reading, writing, and mathematics. They would have group meetings and have identifiable team membership for group projects conducted within the cultural style and manner of Native-American tribal usage. They would bridge the two worlds between Native-American society and mainstream society by gradually creating their own society. But, the theme of all this effort is to advance toward college-level achievement even before the completion of high school. If the students had summer employment for taking classes and conducting projects, the academic results will be accepted for college-level credit. In such a manner, these students would not be wasting their time in school and also they would not be tempted to leave their school community to go to work at minimum-wage levels.

Success breeds success. As these recruited students enter the community college they will be aiming for teacher certification. As they enter the university, they will be completing academic majors for teaching certificates and proof of their successful teaching. They will learn how to create communities of Native-American paraprofessionals to work in Native-American schools. They will become experts in the curriculum development that is necessary if native schools are to succeed as representative of both tribal culture and mainstream culture. Eventually, these teachers will be politically active to build economically secure bases for local rural schools. They will not want to leave such school communities because they will be their own creations. They will be the dominant class and race of their communities; that is, they will own their environment rather than be strangers in a strange land. These results go way beyond the private results for a few individuals; they provide greater possibilities for the whole of society. If a small core of Native-American teachers could so transform community schools, then what would hold back the transformation of higher education in collaboration with American public schools? When students earn their way into a world they can own and live in successfully, then the world we all live in will be enriched.

Conclusion

Returning to Aguerrebere (2003) and his story about going to college as a first-generation student who was dreadfully under-prepared for the post-secondary experience, he told his audience that the purpose of college was to help students from all walks of life break out of their cocoons and experience the joys of life. However, breaking out of the cocoons for those students who live on the margins can seem almost impossible. How the entire nation responds to this crisis of racial and class gaps in education and employment is in one sense a measure of our nation's moral commitment to equity. David Shipler (2004) spells out America's challenge in no uncertain terms: "To appraise a society, examine its ability to be self-correcting. When grievous wrongs are done or endemic suffering exposed, when injustice is discovered or opportunity denied, watch the institutions of government, business and charity. Their response is an index of a nation's health and a people's strength (P. 319)." Robert Putnum (2000) prefers to discuss America's gap in educational and social fairness in terms of what he calls "social capital." "To build bridging social capital requires that we transcend our social and political and professional identities to connect with people unlike ourselves (p. 411)." Confronting marginalization in all its forms—social, educational, and economic and seeking equity—will require all of this nation's resources and strength.

Issues and Questions in Chapter One

Going to college is a big part of the American Dream. But for many it is a nightmare and the questions are:

- Failure rate among marginal groups of college students is over 30 percent, why?
- Marginal is defined not by victim characteristics, but by the treatment minority groups of students receive from educators. How is this related to teachers' expectations?
- Common racial, class and gender specifics of marginal groups of students can be described, but does that explain anything about American Education?
- Why is blaming the victim by society so common and often believed by victims themselves?

  Marginalization and Social Conflict:

- Why is education suspect as a major source of class conflict?
- Are post-modern issues, such as pragmatism, irrelevant to marginal struggling students and, if so, why?
- Why is fear of failure and fear of success in academia common reactions, sometimes among the same students?

Views of the ivory tower: Success results from both luck and work:

- How does academic fortitude increase the likelihood of college success?

- What accounts for the isolation and neglect of marginal students?
- How does plagiarism in Freshman English get used as a sorting device?
- When students lack familiarity of academic codes of conduct disaster follows.
- Isn't it easier to characterize the "race as fixed" in college entrance competition?

What's to be done in higher education?

- Good and early beginnings necessary to recruit college candidates.
- Reduce the price of failure in college.
- Focus on women successes in college.
- Compare with other national systems, e.g. Republic of China educational practices.
- Need for reorganizing the system of higher education.
- Respect for students is invitation to learning.
- Higher Education in Partnership with Secondary Schools requires reaching down to early secondary levels to invite student learning.
- Consider changing the four-year time paradigm for Secondary Schooling.
- Create new partnerships between community colleges and schools.
- We have special programs for talented students, why not for marginal students?
- Vocational/Career Centers are not effective models for marginal students.
- Bay Mills Community College and Ferris State University project, are success examples.

- Overcoming rural isolation for Native Americans takes planning and effort.
- Success in schools leads to commitment to learning in higher education.

"...A wise teacher empties out the clutter
And leaves space for students to fill.
She transforms their ambition
By weakening their desire for approval..."
No. 3. *The Tao of Teaching*

CHAPTER TWO
Access to Higher Education
Introduction

The American aspiration for higher education as a road to a better life for everyone is threatened as a dream turned to nightmare. As the economic and social gap between the upper third of the population and the bottom third widens, so access to better education, especially higher education becomes harder to achieve. The traditional role of hope in the American democratic dream of a just and fair society is being eroded, as increasing numbers of Americans are marginalized, jailed, recruited into military service and consigned to minimal paying jobs. But low paying jobs are not new in American history; what is new is that the hope for higher education and improvement in ones economic and social status is slipping away. The lower expectations result from federal cuts in support for education and for scholarships for higher education. This chapter reviews the conditions which undermine traditional visions of democratic schooling in America. One of the main purposes of education has been to create a more level playing field for everyone, but access to higher education has become more difficult as barriers deter marginalized students from even thinking about college. If this trend continues, it becomes a serious threat to democracy in America.

The international view of America is at extreme odds to the American internal perception of a democratic and just society. Preemptive war in the Middle East did not improve America's image overseas. Americans are tempted to distrust their own beliefs in education as the cure of social injustice. However, for Americans to live without hope for a better and more just world is to accept the invitation to live in either cynicism or despair. Americans love their country and the dream of democracy to an extent that shocks non-Americans. How can we be so naïve? How can we love a country that embraces at once a moral vision of democracy serving all the people and a reality of failure in delivering justice and fairness for all? The gap between wealthy and poor and the gap between comfortable and oppressed is still a wide reality in the United States and it is growing. The distribution of wealth is unequal; urban centers are turned into ghettos for the poor. More and more families are forced to take on two to three jobs in order to meet their financial needs. So, the tax base of the urban school is reduced, precisely at a time when the service needs of the urban citizens have increased (see: Heckman and Krueger, 2003).

Surely, the question must be asked as to why Americans are so against welfare programs, especially those that dispense basic financial support. It is cheaper to supplement income for a family than to support a prisoner in jail. An $18,000. supplement to a family's income is less than half the cost of supporting one prisoner in jail for a year. The costs for prison range between $32,000 to $50,000 per year, per prisoner. Does this make sense? If we were to spend our national wealth on the young we might be able to reverse the gap between rich and poor. However, Americans seem to have a "winner take all mentality" that is inefficient in distribution of wealth. The motto is "the more you win, the more you will win."

Still, Americans live in hope of achieving our democratic vision (Rorty, 1998, p.13). Richard Rorty, argues with Christopher Lasch's (1969) pessimistic view that America is shaping our democracy into an empire. Rorty says such pessimism invites Americans "to stop thinking of oneself as a member of a community, as a citizen with civic responsibilities" (p. 66). If we are to believe the worst of our political life, that we are ineffective in producing positive change, then we are tempted to view our lives as private affairs no longer obliged to serve community betterment. What happens to America when the very word "politics" has a negative connotation? Politics has come to mean self-serving activity, mostly behind the scenes. In fact, the word started its career as a Greek word for "public responsibility" in the open air.

Themes are emerging from the discussion on public responsibility, which argue the competing values of public versus private good. Our current national leadership seems to argue in favor of the priority of the private good, in their funding policies for institutions of higher education and K-12 education. Similarly, states' leadership seems unwilling to view urban centers as deserving of public funding. Cities like Detroit and its citizens are blamed for their own problems and state leadership in Michigan has been hesitant to fund special urban programs badly needed. At a meeting addressing the economic distress around the state, State Senator Michelle McManus spoke about giving money back to the taxpayers. Of course, Detroit/Wayne county would receive the biggest share per person of returned revenue and a majority of those present thought that possibility as awful. What would be a fair level of support of the urban infrastructure? Much of the economic predicament urban centers face come from white leadership moving their businesses and homes out of the cities.

In the United States, public life seems a suspicious arena, but if we are to over-come the gaps between the "haves" and the "have-nots", then public political activity is needed. Cornel West (1999) has written about this dilemma in American democracy:

> *"Hope has nothing to do with optimism. I am in no way optimistic about America, nor am I optimistic about the plight of the human species on this globe. There is simply not enough evidence that allows me to infer that things are going to get better (p. 12)."*

West reminds us that not to hope is to give into despair or cynicism about our country and form of government. To be a citizen in our democracy is to believe, in spite of the evidence to the contrary, that we can make a positive difference in the achievement of justice and fairness for all. Education is the domain where hope is especially the key element. No teacher can teach effectively without believing in spite of the evidence to the contrary that each and every student in her classroom can learn and will learn. Even when there is little reason to support the vision of a morally just society, hope in democracy makes the struggle possible. Again, West tells us that: "To be part of the democratic tradition is to be a prisoner of hope." (Ibid.)

The American vision of a democratic society is given expression in our schools and universities. In spite of the seeming evidence to the contrary, schools in America can be more democratic, providing access and fairness to all students. We hold on to the hope that schools can improve and university access can be more just and fair. Yet, there remains a core of minority students in the American school population who are treated as outsiders to the school success. These students are "marginalized" by the expectations their teachers and by the routine achievement testing required by school administrations. About 25% of the student population is denied access to university admissions because of the failure for these marginalized students to demonstrate academic fortitude. These students are victims of educational discrimination and can be identified mostly as African Americans, Hispanic, Native Americans, and various categories of recent immigrants.

The American educational dilemma is complicated by the probability that if we are to change how schools and colleges treat marginalized students, it will also require that we change how we treat all students. Imagine an academic world that puts the interests of students first and also trusts its students to learn, exercise self-discipline, and govern their own affairs. Currently, most academic institutions put the interests of faculty, administration, and alumni ahead of their students, and as a result create mistrusting environments. Such educational institutions are far from being democratic. Such institutions teach by example that students are not to be trusted, instead of teaching students how to be trustworthy. If there is no trusting, there remains only belief in lies. If we believe that our institutions lie to us routinely, then there is no hope. If there is no hope, nothing can change.

Hope also teaches us that democracy is not a static state, once achieved; but a continuing struggle. To live in a democracy is to be part of the process by which things get done, people are nurtured and cultural diversity is valued. We live in a real world and living so, means we transform the world. Transforming the world in a rewriting of our world, a reconstruction of both who we are and where we live. Non-democratic societies seek to maintain the status quo. Dictators hate change. But democratic societies embrace change. Democratic citizens act as though they are on a wonderful adventure, discovering new realities and surprising possibilities everyday. Therefore, in a democracy the pull toward the future is powerful and feeds our hope that a better, a more just, and equal society will emerge out of the transformation of the world.

Schools can be the agencies of such transformation. That is why Thomas Jefferson knew that a Democratic America required an educated population and that meant public schools for all. Of course, not all the students come to the public school door with the same experience, support and understandings. When one sixth of the school population in America lives in poverty; they do not come to school with the advantage of a full stomach to support the day's activities. So, treating everyone the same is to ignore the differences and to promote and perpetuate the differences in background. Of course, when politicians emphasize treating every one the same, they don't really mean it. They don't want to give up their own specialness; they simply do not want anyone to get an advantage over them. There are national leaders in America who would eliminate "affirmative action" who were admitted to college by receiving special treatment as a legacy applicant. Still, conservative leaders would argue for a simplistic version of democracy where everyone is theoretically "the same."

Let us be clear that our vision of democratic schooling does not mean that everyone is treated the same, studies the same curricula, submits to the same discipline, and accepts the results of meritocracy. The key to democratic schooling is engagement with curriculum. Since schools are about learning, what is learned and how learning takes place are the key issues that must engage all participants in the educational process. Engagement means that students not only have access to the curriculum, but also participate in the creation of the curriculum, its design, its delivery, and its evaluation. Of course, what we are writing about is a much different vision of school than the traditional use of education as the power by which an elite corps of citizens controls the social order. John Dewey in his book *Democracy and Education* argued that education is a process of living now, not a preparation for living sometime down the road. He argues against the notion that pupils are merely candidates for citizenship in the social community; that they were on "the waiting list" of full human beings. The implications of his ideas are tremendous. While students and teachers may not be equals in information, experience and knowledge, they are social and political equals. The school curricula need to offer the variety of students enrolled in any particular school full participation in the current life of the classroom as a basic standard.

Once again, we are confronted with the fact that schools and curricula are very much political domains. Walter Mosley, a novelist and essayist, calls upon the nation to break the chains of yesterday's politics. He writes, "What I want is freedom to share in the incredible wealth of our minds. Let's build a world where progress is for everyone and ownership is for us all. I'm not talking about material ownership here. What I am saying is that our citizens should have equal access to the advantages we discover. Medical care, education, a living wage, and peace of mind should be available for everyone" (2000, p. 106). One cannot write about curricula without writing about politics, economics and community values. Richard Allington, speaking at Ferris State University, addressed this theme that the poor and marginalized are more dependent on the school resources than their affluent counterparts in the suburbs. Consequently, any change in the curricula of urban schools will have to occur though political processes.

During the current Middle East war, we read about a town in rural Northern Michigan with a population of 400 people. Sixty of the young people from this town are away in the military services and most are fighting in a far away, arid land. The reason a high percentage of the town is in the military is that there are no jobs in this small town. So, the young poor seek employment in the U.S. military and end up doing the fighting for the rest of us. The rich do not go to war. The rich send others to war to do their dirty work. For example, when asked why she joined the armed forces, a young Native American woman and mother answered, "It's a job." Subsequently, she died in the war.

Writing school curricula creates possibilities that can transform society. Paulo Freire, Brazil's prophetic philosopher and educator, had a vision of a democratic curriculum that would transform people by putting them on the road to security and peace. His vision included the possibility of living without violence. Schools would be truly public space that could be used by all the people of the community. People could find a balance between life and work that would construct relationships among people. Citizenship would be a cherished status; getting it and keeping it would be a valuable commodity. According to Freire's vision, schools would be connected intimately to the neighborhood and Freire understood that access to education also meant economic access. A democratic curriculum requires students, staff, teachers, specialist, and parents to come together and work together. Freire said: "We should not call on the people to come to school to receive instruction, recipes, threats, reprehension, and punishment, but to participate collectively in the construction of knowledge" (p. 169 Macedo, 1994). From Freire's point of view a canned curriculum cannot possibly cover all a local people's needs. Furthermore, if school curricula truly served the needs of everyone, then all secondary school graduates would be prepared for the rigors of college curricula. But the fact remains that marginalized students come to college unprepared; they lack process and content knowledge; they are easily distracted; and they lack tenacity. (Levine & Cureton, 1998) When marginalized students go to college they also have additional priorities other than school. Going to school is just one of their priorities. They have to make a living, they have families, and they live very complex lives for the same age as their mainstream counterparts. Their concerns are local and focus on survival. They do not possess a global perspective and they usually have not traveled much.

North Central Regional Education Laboratory (NCREL) describes engaged learning as a changing of roles such that the students and teachers become co-learners and co-developers of curriculum. When teachers and students participate together in meaningful tasks, the teaching and the learning and assessment become seamless, as do the divisions of authority. The in-class and out-of-class dynamic of traditional learning disappears.

What would define a quality undergraduate education for these marginalized students? The answer is what we expect for all undergraduate students. Students would come to college with high expectations for success. The college would respect their diverse talents and perspectives; but would emphasize in the early years of study: coherence between what they are learning formally and synthesizing experiences of the college environment. Students would engage in practice-learned skills; they would integrate experience and education. Through out the early years of college students would see the connections between active learning with assessment and planned feedback. They would know how to plan for and provide adequate time on learning tasks. But most of all, they would have contact with faculty both in and out of class to engage in the long term discourse about knowledge and its uses.

One example of such organized learning environments is Saxion Hogeschool in Enschede, the Netherlands. First year business students form teams and must start a commercial business. Their instructors act as consultants to their business projects. After they complete the first year, the students study theory, research, and knowledge base in the field, both on and off campus. This learning model engages the students, who can see why they need to read, write, compute and analyze more formally.

There are lots of resources that describe what sorts of quality education models work in schools. The work of P. A. Alexander in *Educational Researcher* (March 2000), "Toward a Model of Academic Development: Schooling and Knowledge Acquisition," provides an excellent example of a research-based educational model. Her work is one of many advocating sane and sound educational curriculum reform. The question one must ask is: if resources like these actually provide knowledge about the structure of a quality education, what stops America from creating these conditions for all students? Many teachers still expect students to think like they do, do as they do, feel as they do. When one accepts the invitation to be like someone else, this creates a sense of dependency and helplessness. Dependencies and failures, in turn, create anxiety. Anxiety created by the challenge of learning in a hostile environment, can produce generations of Americans with fear of intellectual engagement and formal learning.

Coping with the demands of college is not the same as coping with constructing understandings from experience. Many colleges, as a result, have been transformed from places of study and growth to platforms for credentialing. David Labaree (1997) argues that the connection between schooling and social mobility has transformed colleges and universities from educational institutions to credentialing institutions. "I argue that we need to back away from the whole idea that getting ahead should be the central goal of education (p.1). One could also argue that as college continue to foster fear of failure with genuine intellectual engagement, students find a substitute for the purpose of education and that would be in the acquisition of educational credentials. Labaree calls the paraphernalia of academic documentation "symbolic goods, such as grades, credits, and degrees." He writes, "The urge to get ahead has transformed the basic function of U.S. education from public service to private service, and this transformation has brought significant consequences for the people who attend, work in, pay for, and in various ways depend on American schools" (p. 258).

The atmosphere of credentialing undermines the learning itself. If the goal of education is a degree and a job, then the substance of the study will seem irrelevant. If college is basically a means for acquiring a job after the degree is awarded, then it makes suspect the struggle and effort needed to acquire understandings and skills. Furthermore, credentialing will reinforce the injustice of class distinctions in the acquisition of credits and degrees. Whenever people are sorted by pre-existing conditions, whether it is merit or class, IQ or health, ethnic or gender characteristics, the achievements of genuine knowledge, understandings and skills are undervalued and class warfare prospers. Education that does not empower students perpetuates old class distinctions and breeds a sense of failure and wasted time in school and colleges.

The concept of democratic schooling raises the specter of a confrontation between the tyranny of meritocracy and the price of compensatory college education. Should we pay college level costs for remediation when public primary schools fail to educate? This is certainly not a smart or economic public policy. We participate in a system of public schools, especially at the primary levels, which is controlled by local communities, usually within the county. There is a bias at this level against spending money on poor people, particularly their schooling. So, they just don't teach them to read and do math. It is rarely a public debate. How it works is that school boards hire the youngest, least experienced teachers, especially if they are graduates of their own local schools. So, they perpetuate the cycle of poor teaching and the neglect of the rural poor. Families who do not get any attention to their educational needs can receive the same treatment from the school faculty across generations. So, many American adults cannot read. How did they get that way in a society of required public schooling? How can they graduate without being able to read? How can we now pay for compensatory college education to teach them to read? Richard Allington, education professor and literacy advocate in Florida, is right to say that the poor are more dependent on schools for their success than the privileged. It is hard to explain why schools do not teach the poor to read?

Perhaps it is simply because the local primary school districts are not willing to pay for the expertise that can teach anyone to read. What success ill-trained and inexperienced teachers do have, appears to come from those children of families that already taught their own children how to read. Schools become for the advantaged children an arena for demonstrating their skills and understanding. No wonder that the poor are amazed at the success of the advantage students! No wonder that the poor blame themselves for their failures! It seems to the poor that the rich kids just are so much better people, so much better readers, better students, healthier, etc. So, the poor often end up muttering to themselves, "There's something wrong with me, doomed to failure, because I am dumb!"

The fact of the matter is that we are not equal and to pretend that we are is to pretend a lie. Democratic schools must acknowledge that we are all different. We have different experiences and we have different skills, and we receive different treatment. Teachers naturally believe in separating the "slow" from the so-called "creative" students; then they spend as much of the time as they can with the bright and creative students. We want to believe that every teacher wants the best for all students. We will believe it when we can see all students clearly receiving teachers' best efforts according to each student's need.

However, the practice of tracking students into groups based on reading levels has been an insidious practice that flies in the face of consistent evidence that being placed in a "low reading group" almost never leads to reaching the higher level groups. Most of the time tracking is a device that makes life easier for the teacher. Tracking as a commonly recommended strategy was abandoned by the profession in the 1970s, it is still to be found in many classrooms. Cunningham and Allington

(2003) show that there is research which demonstrates the negative effects of tracking students by achievement levels (p. 262). They remind us that if schools are to prepare students to participate in our democratic society, they must help create the conditions in which students can learn and work together with many students from a variety of backgrounds and levels of understanding. Carl Glickman (1998) says, "The practice of tracking in subtle and not-so-subtle ways to separate students by race, class, and family background can be found in other schools and districts across the United States (p. 165)."

The issue for democratic schooling is establishing the threshold at which citizens may fully participate in the democratic process. Amy Gutmann argues that "the content of education should be reoriented toward teaching students the skills of democratic deliberation (p. 171)." In other words, democratic schooling requires the differential of students because each has different thresholds for participation in public discussion. However, the demands for democratic schooling go beyond the schoolhouse. More must be done by society to create jobs for the poor, decent housing, medical and childcare. Without the good faith effort of governments and businesses within communities to raise the level of support for the poor and dispossessed, America will remain at class warfare between the haves and the have nots.

The demands of democratic schooling, therefore, lead us deeply into economic issues. When American businesses move their headquarters to islands off the shores of the mainland (Bermuda, for example) in order to avoid paying local and federal taxes, they are telling their fellow Americans that paying taxes is a fool's choice. We wrote to a business that had announced a move to Bermuda, accusing the board of being irresponsible citizens, interested only in profits. They company wrote back saying we were just being naive. If the company did not stay competitive, they felt they would have to go out of business, because every one of their competitors were making their profits from overseas bases of operation. Who is being naïve? When companies contribute to the disintegration of the social order by undermining economic stability in their communities, how can they expect to continue to sell their products to Americans who eventually will be unable to afford their products.

Sending the jobs overseas is not merely an economic issue. It is a social issue and ultimately an educational issue. When the economy slides, the schools will suffer and become unable to fulfill the demands of democratic schooling. Many cities in America are so stretched economically, that they cannot afford to maintain their schools at effective levels of operation. This fact along can account for much of the movement of the middle class out of the urban centers to suburban communities who offer better schools and safer streets. Of course, this becomes a cycle, as the middle and upper classes move out to the suburbs, the tax base for the urban centers erodes, providing even less resources to the public schools. The same story can be told about rural America. As the small, family farm has failed to provide the economic stability for rural counties, and as small businesses have left the rural settings, the tax resources for the schools narrow down. Schools were consolidated and students spent long hours on buses to attend central school facilities. But when the students of rural schools graduate, they leave the community, first for universities for those who choose that route, and finally to find the jobs to support their lives. A large majority of the rural population who leave for the jobs and a so called "better life," never return. The result leaves the rural communities even more depleted, as the most successful of the school graduates are the most successful in finding employment and a decent living elsewhere. The tax base thins again; and the school budget suffers. Also, the possibilities of genuine education and academic achievement suffer. One rural Michigan school board member commented recently to us that without jobs and no hope for the future, students are not motivated in their school work and express the view that "everything is a waste of time."

Even while we explore ideas of democratic schooling, there are threats to the institution of democracy in America. Zakaria has recently published his views as to the weaknesses in United States democracy. He claims that, "America is increasingly embracing a simple-minded populism that values popularity and openness as the key measures of legitimacy...The result is a deep imbalance in the American system, more democracy but less liberty" (Niall Ferguson, 4/13/03, p. 9). What critics of American democracy, like Zarkaria, are pointing to is the increasing dependence of government and its agencies on professional lobbyists and wealthy campaign contributors to the political process. Corruption and fraud are the consequences of government run by close personal associations away from public scrutiny. At many levels, the role of lobbyists and personal connections seem to dominate governmental decisions in the United States. For example, in Florida, the Governor and the legislature have fallen under the influence of the publishers of the *Phonics Teaching* methods for teaching reading. They have required all teachers in Florida schools to use the textbooks published by these businesses, and have all the teachers take phonics methods training, even though teaching phonics has nothing to do with a student learning to read! At every level of government one can find the influence of lobbyists and pressure groups. Rules and regulations are shaped by agencies under the influence of private perspectives rather than publicly tested values discussed and air in forums, town halls, and election campaigns.

The distinctions between the curricular options of the affluent students versus the marginalized students are impressive. Affluent students have the newest technology and come from environments where they are surrounded by books, have access to technology, participate in enriching activities and travel, and learn that expectations for their academic success are high throughout their education. Not so, for the marginalized students. For example, in the elite private schools affluent students "shop" and decide which instructors offer the best classes for them. While in the urban public schools, marginalized students have to pay fines if they drop a class or change sections.

Who chooses the textbooks in American schools? Many teachers will report that a committee appointed by the principal or superintendent make recommendations to the board of education. But the fact of the matter is that the majority of textbook decisions are made in California and Texas, where these states have statewide adoption policies. The textbook adoption committees of these states are such big customers of the textbook companies that whatever these two states want in terms of content gets published. The lobbying and pressures from special groups is powerful (Ravitch, 2003). Even at the district or state level of decision making, these decisions are made under the heavy influence and pressure from the publishing firms and the various community groups that share a particular perspective. So, history books have to present the appropriate version of the Civil War, or the Woman's suffrage movement, as seen by the pressure groups. There is, therefore, a constant tendency in a democracy to have decisions on policy and programs influenced by friendly voices. That is the nature of an open system. As a result, democratically elected governments are periodically overturned, ("throw the bums out!") and new officials installed. Such turn-overs, or purges, help to keep governments from becoming too corrupt over time. Still, many a school board has elected members who have served for decades and the longer they stay in office the more dangerous they become.

Many people believe that colleges are designed for the privileged and wealthy. A growing number of people also believe that colleges and universities are havens of liberalism and left-wing craziness. Sending a son or daughter to college could permanently damage them. Our father believed in education and affirmed the idea that college ought to be socially useful, as in providing the training, skills and understandings to get a job and make a contribution to the community, but still he respected the hard work necessary to achieve the recognition that a college degree brings! On the other hand, writers like Paul Goodman (1962) wrote of "the community of scholars" seeking knowledge for its own sake, without any definable social utility. These two views of the purpose of education provide an insight into the nature of democratic schooling. Schools do provide the tools for social engagement in the democratic processes; also they support the spiritual journey of self-discovery. Both the practical needs of society and the inspirational needs of individuals are served by a democratic education. It would be foolish to insist that schools and colleges exist only to provide trained workers for employment in the next generation of technical institutions. Likewise, it would be naïve to pursue knowledge for its own sake with no social responsibility. All knowledge has its social and political consequences. To know something is not merely a private event, though its acquisition often is, but also a public event linked to the social order. So, one cannot argue successfully for long that schooling is a private journey designed for individuals to discover their personal identity. Such exercises in learning would be superficial if they do not result in participation in the struggle for a more just and humane social and economic order (Cf. Chomsky, 2003, pp. 298 ff.)

The student movements of the 1960s and 70s shook the ivory tower of university life, which was complacent and isolated from social and economic realities. Before the radical changes of the Vietnam era, many people assumed that the role of colleges and universities was to replicate the previous generation, thereby continuing the social and economic order. On the other hand, it was tempting for scholars to isolate themselves from society and, in many cases; their students in order to explore more and more narrow fields of investigation. Universities were also threatened by the concept of classified research, which brought rich federal grants to university campuses, but challenged the open sharing essential to the sciences. The rebellious students called the academic world accountable for doing research to bring more sophistication to the bombing of Southeast Asian villages; while at the same time the inner cities of North America were rotting socially and economically.

Higher education continues to struggle with issues of purpose and the appropriate use of resources to achieve their goals. David Kirp (2003) describes in detail how many universities have become large entrepreneurial establishments, rewarding professors who bring in the grants and contracts to enrich the coffers of the campus. Often undergraduates at such universities rarely get to see much less take a class from a full professor, as many who teach the undergraduate courses are temporary instructors outside of the tenure system or poorly trained graduate assistants who teach to support the own graduate studies. Still, there remain colleges who pride themselves in serving the undergraduate students, offering a more general educational recipe of courses. Professors in these small colleges take pride in their teaching, but they often are cut off from the large professional associations and from the current research in their field. These colleges are often private and very expensive to attend. Some hold high standards for intellectual engagement by their students, but some offer narrowly focused courses with religious or political orientations. There are so many types of institutions of higher education it is genuinely difficult for the public to know how to interpret the institutional missions of each. The wide range of differences include public versus private; non-sectarian versus religious; poor versus rich; elitist versus service orientation programs; engineering versus humanities orientations; large multiversities versus small liberal arts colleges; and city colleges versus rural institutions. Given such diversity, it is a dangerous path to walk by offering generalizations about the values and practices of higher education. Yet, it still must be done to discuss our visions of democratic schooling.

The role of a university is seen differently by political conservatives and their corresponding political liberals. The conservative interpreter of the university mission is to maintain traditional knowledge and serve the public as first, the researcher for new inventions, and second, the training academy for the experts needed to run the country in both business and government. The liberal interpreter of universities sees them as the "free marketplace of ideas." The liberal believes in the free society and the university is the pillar of the free society. Ideas should be explored and their consequences weighed openly and freely. Once this freedom is infringed upon by coercion to consider only a few ideas or a restricted set of ideas, the university loses its value to a free society. So the dilemma of university reform is much the same as public school reform: if curriculum is forced upon the faculty, then the freedom of ideas fails. Teachers at every level must believe in the autonomy of their own ideas and be willing to live with the consequences of them. This is the very nature and characteristic of professional standards. Once teaching becomes a walking through and reading of a script, written by someone else, it ceases to be teaching and becomes slave labor. Likewise, teachers lose the battle of leadership when they coerce their own students to be like them, believe their beliefs, and think as they do. Without the joint engagement of minds meeting minds, there is only dictatorial programming, not invitations to leaning and understanding.

The art of teaching itself is like leading a democratic community. Each participant has a voice in the proceedings; expressing ones voice is central to the nature of democracy. This does not mean that some members of the school academy do not know more, both qualitatively and quantitatively, than others. Some people have more experience, are older, stronger than others. In a participating democracy, however, there is common caring for the good of the whole, as well as the welfare of the individual. We are talking about all levels of school when we apply this principle. So, prescriptive reform movements do not work in academic communities.

But once again, Americans face a serious dilemma at this point. The agencies of government in Washington and the state capitols must layout requirements for school districts in the treatment of handicapped students. And there are a bundle of lay-on mandates that state and federal governments require of schools and universities. Regulations as to how the academy should be managed, how students should be treated, how safety issues must be addressed, how fairness and just treatment of all students must be applied, all these are required of the central government. It is the job of government to regulate for the good of all its citizens. And yet, many schools and colleges chaff under the unfunded mandates that are laid on them. The recourse of the political process is the most obvious cure. Schools can lobby as well as big business. School districts can start up political campaigns; they do have their effects. The avoidance of politics and lobbying by teachers and administrators is often justified by appeals to so-called higher plains of professional endeavor. But it is not beneath teachers and administrators to engage in democratic politics. To avoid such engagement is to pledge some distrust to the democratic process itself.

We urge not merely tolerance of the political process, we urge the academy at every level to expect and support "action informed by reason." Still, some educators take pride in being apolitical. The fact is there is no such thing as apolitical positions; because to take no action when the political issues heat up and the politicians take up their causes, is to concede the field to those politicians ready to fight for what they believe in or profit from. Therefore, to be apolitical is to be a supporter of the "let some one else do it" syndrome. When the race begins we must join in, run, walk, hobble, jog, what ever. But to refuse to walk, to sit on the sidelines, is to cheer those who will take the risks of running the race. A democracy requires an engaged citizenry.

The answers to questions about marginalized students and what must be done to improve their educational experience within the academy may be found in the political arena. Paulo

Freire's vision of education as the "practice of freedom" speaks volumes about the failures of educational reform movements in America. Some would have us believe that the answer to school reform is to be found in educational technology. But even Bill Gates of Microsoft has admitted that distributing free computers to people who are hungry and in need of medical care does not help the poor. In America, much of what poses as answers to the problems of school reform has been extensions of positivism in school materials and methodologies. Little will be reformed without the rethinking that comes from political engagement in democracy; again, because the political sphere is linked to the educational process. Teaching and the quality of its consequences are joined to the social and economic problems affecting the school academy. The fact is that most teachers in America avoid political, social, or economic commentary with their students and their parents and for good reason, as they have learned that politics and the schoolhouse do not mix easily in American communities. However, this aversion to political action on the part of educators subverts any chance for their students to become fully engaged community citizens unless they inherit their political standing from their parents.

We believe the majority of teachers in America are good citizens and carry the best of intentions into their classrooms. Yet, most teachers do not see their work as political work and would refuse to accept any responsibility for such a position. Talk to the teachers in any school in America about the need for school reform and what you get are two responses: what is needed is: 1) better students and 2) better administrators with more funding support for teachers. The students are blamed by teachers for their own, supposed inadequacies. Likewise, teachers accuse uncaring administrators and under funding of the school budgets as causing problems. However, to accuse these two sources for school failure is how teachers let themselves off the hook of professional responsibility.

Numerous educational groups represent teachers, administrators, educational researchers, teacher educators, and school boards. Teachers are represented by National Education Association (NEA) or American Federation of Teachers (AFT). Other groups representing curriculum and special subjects like the Association for Supervision and Curriculum Development (ASCD) or the National Council of Teacher Educators (NCTE). There are specific groups representing educational research, American Educational Research Association (AERA) and American Psychological Association (APA) and groups representing teacher educators, American Association of Colleges of Teacher Education (AACTE) or Association of Teacher Educators (ATE). All these and many more groups at all levels of education have annual conferences and they are constantly talking about and feature issues on educational reform. Why does not all this activity produce reform? The answer is because they do not engage in the political process in a democratic society. Americans have become deeply suspicious of politics, politicians and elections. The very term "political" is seen as a negative concept. "Don't become involved with politics," we say. Yet, there is no other answer to question of school reform and the restructuring of higher education. It must be a political process.

The democratic political process is based on evolution (step by step social reconstruction) until things get so bad that they require revolution. We do not believe we have reached revolutionary levels of institutional failure, as yet. Still, even acknowledging many school successes every day, much that happens in schools must be failure. And the problem seems to be that the failures happen most regularly and most tragically with the marginalized community. One out of six public school students lives in poverty. One out of four black American males under 25 are in jail in our urban centers. The problems of the homeless, the jobless, and the medical careless find their expressions in the public school community. There remain wide domains for school reform.

Literature concretizes the human arena inviting the reader's imaginative ownership (learning) to engage in the thinking process. Thinking and dreaming go hand in hand and produce "action informed by reason." Mechanical and material solutions apply to some problems; namely, those problems that are material by nature, i.e. quantitative. However, most of the problems of education are qualitative; they call out for imaginative and humane solutions. This is why liberal arts college graduates are so much in demand, because they know how to do their own thinking and use their imagination. Liberal education and democracy both embrace the open discussion of ideas from any quarter. Reading Karl Marx one day and Ralph Waldo Emerson another day is like listening to a town hall democratic debate. Freedman writes about the value of preserving the liberal arts in the academy at two levels. First, the liberal arts lead individuals to self-understanding, but secondly... "Liberal education in America is also about understanding the foundations of a democratic society and appreciating the responsibilities of citizenship" (2003, pp.64-65). The liberal arts inspire the mind by transforming it. Reading Richard Wright's *Native Son* transports one to the slums of Chicago and the experiences of an African American with all the issues of poverty and racism and ethnicity. Likewise, music and the plastic arts can transport us to new realms for the imagination. The stirring of the soul and mind prepares on for the public arena of democratic institutions and frees us from the burdens of easy ideas and con artists who would convince one that cutting the public taxes is the only way to raise money for improving the economy, for example. Because, in a democracy there is always a competing voice over how the public welfare should be served. That debate must be conducted openly and fairly, or the consequences are that public power becomes the private domain of a few and inevitably the few are always the money class. We need a democratic education to assure the cause of free and open public schools.

William Ayers makes the charge that the "standards movement" pushed by the political conservatives is a "fraud" (Ayers, 2000). The students, Ayers points out, whom the movement toward accountability standards punish are overwhelmingly the poor, the urban poor, the students of color (Latino and African-American students. For example, Ayers reports that in Chicago over a two-year period over 50,000 kids attended summer school in the name of standards. In Florida (2003), 15,000 seniors will not graduate with their classmates, because they failed to pass FCAT. Again, the predominate portion of this student population are African American and Hispanics. Ayers, raises the issue of democracy in the midst of the standards pressures for "school reform." He writes: "The purpose of education in a democracy is to break down barriers, to overcome obstacles, to open doors, minds, and possibilities." *(pp. 67)*

From the K-12 public schools to the colleges and universities the call to American democratic roots is increasingly insistent. The shift in emphasis of the last decades of the twentieth century in higher education has been toward professional education. Professionalism is the university's answer to the students' shift of interest toward seeing education as the means of "getting a job" (Rhodes, 2001). Professionalism moves the curriculum from a liberal arts education to specialized training programs. In training programs knowledge is often treated as a commodity that one acquires in order to be admitted to some specialization. The practical economic consequences of specializing early seemed to be justified by the high costs of higher education. The sooner one is credentialed, the sooner one starts earning a living instead of preparing for a livelihood. Or so, it has been thought by many.

However, the credentialed approach does not seem to have worked as a pragmatic scheme to professional success. Medical schools, for example, have found out that pre-medical undergraduates who specialized early in the laboratory sciences made particularly insensitive interns and then doctors. Now, many medical schools are looking for the more broadly liberal arts educated undergraduates to study medicine. Interestingly, music majors have had particular success in acceptance rates in medical schools.

The specialization implied in university professional courses creates serious educational problems. As knowledge becomes more specialized, individual faculty become less and less humane as their scope or vision narrows. As a result the value of the liberal arts as a broad higher education perspective seems to diminish in the eyes of some faculty. Faculty who become increasingly specialized in their field of expertise also become increasingly ignorant of the larger issues of living morally in a diverse society. The university has an obligation to serve the public in the pursuit of both general knowledge and specialized knowledge. The latter without the former makes for moral pigmies. Unless we do pursue the larger visions of public service, the people who support higher education with their taxes will have their anti-intellectualism confirmed by the actions of the academy.

There is also a link between a broad liberal arts education and democratic discourse. Democracy demands the kind of open discourse that is supported by a background in the liberal arts. University major fields of study that are firmly embedded in the humanities tradition, and we include the basic science fields as humanities disciplines, provide the experience and content of thinking skills and information that make one unlikely to be easily persuaded by facile arguments, based on whims or extremes. In political discourse there are always those who will try to flim-flam others into believing their own moral make-believes. It takes a liberal arts or humanities education to sort out the con artists from the sincere political advocates.

At Michigan State University, the Teacher Education Department some years ago was concerned with the number of elementary education majors that had no roots in the academic disciplines of the university. Many of the elementary education majors were ill informed about the basics in mathematics, sciences, and literature, and yet they were training to become the first teachers of children in elementary schools. So, the department changed the requirements for receiving teacher certification from MSU in Michigan, by adding an intern year (a fifth year) and requiring an academic undergraduate major as a prerequisite for the intern year. This move changed the playing field decisively. Those who elected teacher certification at MSU, became majors in the several academic departments of school related subjects and had to participate in a full year of graduate studies and internship in teaching. No longer were the students who chose this path to a teaching career in the lowest percentile of the university admissions for each class. Prior to this curriculum change, one could count on entering freshman majors in elementary education to be in the lowest 20% of the university admission class. This fact has been recognized by the people who developed the admissions testing programs, like SATs. Lemann describes how the standardized tests showed early on the "lowest scorers by far were the very people who were going to be entrusted with this benighted system (i.e. public education) in the future...education majors" (2000, p. 22).

Even if one has grave doubts about the usefulness of standardized tests, I.Q. tests and various achievement tests, (Educational Testing Service (ETS), College Entrance Examination Board (CEEB), Graduate Record Examination (GRE), etc.) and we do have doubts, the record was clear that public schools are not hiring teachers who were at the top of the college classes in achievement on such tests. Therefore, the profession of teaching suffers from ill-educated and unprepared practitioners of classroom leadership. The majority of teachers have been unprepared to lead their students into the arena of democratic learning environments, much less actually engage in democratic discourse. How could democratic schools be created if the majority of teachers were afraid of politics and unprepared to debate the critical issues of democratic participation in the school curriculum? Something more needs to change if the American Dream of Democratic schooling is to be achieved and access to higher education is to be available to all American students.

Issues and Questions for Chapter Two

Prisoners of Hope:
- Why does Cornel West define the moral obligations of democratic citizens in terms of "Prisoners of Hope?"
- How can those American school children who live in poverty be described as having hope?
- What will it take to bring justice to the American school system?
- Visions of a better world and better schooling for all come from what personal resources?

Educational Transformation:
- How can education which offers so much freedom, also be used as power to control the social order?
- How can Paulo Freire's vision of a democratic curriculum include work and leisure?
- Build a road to security?
- Create the possibility of living without violence?
- Can people use of space in schools for constructing relationships, enhancing citizenship? Community, conviviality, consciousness and transformation produce neighborhoods?
- How can we think of access to education as also economic access?

Creation of Culture Confirms Competence:
- A canned curriculum created some other place, by some other educators, cannot possibly cover everyone's needs!

- Students, staff, teachers, specialist, parents must come together to create a democratic curriculum.
- People construct knowledge, local people build local knowledge.
- How can marginalized students succeed in college if they enter unprepared?
- In contrast with mainstream students, marginalized students go to college with many other priorities and obligations from attending school.

Quality Undergraduate Education

- Quality in College include the skills of academic fortitude: Describe some of the main characteristics of academic fortitude.
- Coping with the demands of college are not the same as coping with constructing understandings from experience.
- Explain how colleges have been transformed from places of study and growth to platforms for credentialing.
-

"...Using knowledge as a club to rule,
Robs the people of confidence,
And corrupts institutions.
When people know how little they know,
The community needs no poll takers.
They at least know a poll
Is a collection of ignorance..."
No. 65 *The Tao of Teaching*

CHAPTER THREE
Schooling for All

Nicholas Lemann has written an engaging and important book, *The Big Test: The Secret History of the American Meritocracy* (2000). He tells the story of the development of the SAT test for college admissions and the politics behind required testing. Basically, the story centers on the efforts of the Harvard University president of the mid-20th century, James Bryant Conant, to establish reliable criteria for admissions to college other than being a member of the upper class and a legacy applicant. Dr. Conant, a chemistry professor, had an extreme aversion to rich students who were representatives of the undemocratic elite in American and whose fathers ran the corporations and government agencies. He wanted a system that would create a scientific basis for selecting the most talented and energetic young men in the country to go to college. Within a few years, Dr. Conant and his associates were fabulously successful changing the college admissions system from one based on an elite of wealth and privilege, to an elite of talent and accomplishment.

From a relative small group of admissions deans and testing psychologists, there came a series of achievement tests. Over their history, the American College Testing (ACT) in Iowa and the Scholastic Aptitude Test (SAT) at Educational Testing Service (ETS) in Princeton, New Jersey, have become tremendous influences on the public high school curriculum. Students had to take these tests in order to get into college, much less be considered for a scholarship. Therefore, high schools had to offer the kind of courses that would prepare the students to compete successfully on these tests. ETS described the SAT as measure of "scholastic aptitude." Many interpreted this concept as a close relative of IQ and reported, therefore, how "brainy" a student was. The ACT was described as a test of academic achievement. Between the two almost every student in America was tested for college admissions from the 1950s onward. Success on these tests identified the student as an applicant most likely to succeed in college courses. The most successful usually had a choice among several colleges and scholarships. Students with high SAT scores could elect to go to colleges of their preference. Meanwhile, students who did not have high scores had to fight to have any "choice" at all to get a college education.

Recently, there has been a tendency to flatten out the ACT and the SAT test scores. *The Wall Street Journal* reports that the emphasis on high stakes testing by the states and national leadership has reduced the time spent on college level preparation courses. (Kronholz, 2003). Students just are not taking enough higher level courses or follow the recommended high school curriculum for college admissions. The emphasis is gradually changing to scoring well on state generated high school graduation tests. The marginalized students tend to pull down the average school scores and are often deleted from the final school test results.

Students from all corners of the country, however, from urban centers, the poor, African-American, Hispanic, Native-Americans, immigrants, rural poor and the handicapped were neglected and marginalized in schools and compromised in their efforts to reach for higher education opportunities. These marginalized students are diverse in backgrounds, interests, and experiences; but most of them have been miss-educated to believe that there really was a world of privileged, private knowledge from which they are denied access by virtue of their academic failure. It is bad enough to fail an academic course, but to fail and believe your failure is the result of your being a bad or unworthy person is tragic. When civil rights legislation was enacted by Congress, affirmative action was created by President Lyndon Johnson's Executive Order 11246 on September 24, 1965. Still, over the following decades, marginalized students had to struggle to exercise a choice of higher education. Changing the definition of the elite class from one of class privilege to one of ability and achievement did not change the basic conflict between the rich and the poor, between easy access to higher education and struggled access.

The leadership of the country in the 20th century evolved into an elite class of lawyers, doctors, bankers, professors, and accountants. Early in the century, this educated class was held in high regard, but the closing years of the century has seen the trust and prestige of the professions wear thin. Fraud, huckstering, and selfish behavior have become common place. Who would have thought that the CEOs of democracy's largest corporations would defraud the shareholders and milk the company for wealth and personal benefits! America is for sale, seems to be the current motto of our national leadership.

In no area is the perversion of American leadership more evident than in the demand for educational accountability through testing. Turn to Texas to find the origins of testing to defraud Americans of equal educational opportunities. Peter Sacks describes the Texas Assessment of Academic Skills as a ... "state-sanctioned punishment of its poor and minority school children, flunking them on the basis of a standardized test." (1999, p. 110). The Mexican-American Legal Defense Educational Fund (MALDEF) filled suit in San Antonio in 1997 charging that "The Texas Education Agency had severely punished Texas minorities by flunking them, retaining them, and tracking them into substandard 'drill and kill' instruction programs, completely disregarding a student's actual classroom performance." *(p. 111)*

In effect, Sacks describes the state of Texas as two Texases. One Texas is designed for the elite and economically comfortable community, and the other Texas is left to deal with the African-American and Hispanic communities living in poverty. So, if one wishes to find the division in American democracy, one only has to turn to the public schools to discover the deep divide in the heart of Texas. Tests are touted as the vehicle for improving schools by finding a base for accountability among schools. But the tests divide between class and race by consequence if not by intention. Only half of the Mexican American and African-American students who took the TAAS passed it, while eight in ten white students passed it. (Ibid.) These tests have become the banner of the current "No Child Left Behind" movement, still they have yet to prove anything but the deep marginalization of about a quarter of the American population. The results demonstrate the failure of America to educate one out of four Americans, while at the same time blaming these victims of incompetent schooling.

Teachers may insist that parents are to blame for their students' poor performances on tests of achievement. Teachers claim that their "hands are tied" and parents do not risk the power they have to change the system that teachers say they are stuck in. Ruben Navarrette, a reporter on the staff of *The Dallas Morning News*, writes about the results of a recent comprehensive survey of Texas public schools. (2003). What was found, Navarrette reports, is that the schools with the highest number of poor and minority students were least likely to have highly qualified and experienced teachers. Navarrette tells us that based on the survey of 7,000 schools, a teacher preparation index was created by combining the percentage of teachers who were certified; the percentage of teachers who were certified and teaching in the subject area specialty; and the percentage of teachers with at least two years' experience. The scale was 1 to 10. What was found was that if a school had "a student body of more than 90 percent white, the rating was 6.3. For schools that were largely Latino, the average was 4.6. For those mostly black, the figure was 3.4 percent." In other words, poor and minority students are stuck with less trained and less experienced teachers. Those with the most need for help in English language skills and other basic skills were provided with the least qualified teachers. This phenomenon does not happen without careful planning on somebody's part. Somehow, those who make decisions for schools as to which schools get the best teachers constantly place the highest qualified teachers in classrooms where academic achievement is already at a high level.

Two results seem most obvious with regard to the national testing for school accountability movement: one is that teachers and schools have learned to teach *to* the tests if they want bonuses (as in the Florida Comprehensive Assessment Test FCAT, program); the second result is that marginalized students are denied access to higher education. If students do not pass the senior level tests they do not graduate from high school and are not eligible for admission to higher education options, no matter what the student accomplishes in the classrooms. In 2003, Florida found that 15,000 high school students did not pass the FCAT with high enough scores to graduate. Also, 43,000 third-grade students around the state failed to pass the reading test and are facing retention. Even though educational research results are clear that holding back as an educational strategy does not work, the Florida Education Department rejects such research as "goobley-gook."

What is proclaimed as raising standards for public education turns out to be a scam, weeding out the unworthy and creating a permanent welfare and criminal community subculture. If people have no options, they have no standing in the democratic community which surrounds them. There is some suspicion that the phrase, "No Child Left Behind," is actually a prediction that they will be left behind, especially if Florida's experience in high states testing is a fair example. The majority of the failures on these tests are poor and minority students. One is tempted to believe that the purpose of the No Child Left Behind law is precisely to weed out the failures in the system, because tests do not teach.

The strategy of laying out painful consequences for failure to meet standards, such as awarding bonuses for successful schools and loss of accreditation to failing schools, is called "high-stakes testing." The metaphor references the gambling casinos where high rollers bet high stakes of money on the "crap shoot." And that is about as fitting a description of these multiple choice tests as one can imagine. These tests are a kind of gamble. The bonuses are supposed to offer teachers and schools incentives for high achievements. But the punishments implied by not achieving high scores create an environment of fear. Visit a school about to take the tests. Do it before the test-taking days because schools often will not allow outsiders to enter the building on testing days. Listen to the panic among the students and the fear in the voices of teachers. If you do, you will understand why the resistance to testing programs is a growing phenomenon across the country. Taking a test is neither fun nor educational. What is learned by taking tests is that knowledge is measured by information bytes that can be displayed in multiple-choice options. If that is what knowledge is, who needs it? When we live in a fearful environment and are threatened by punishments of failure, the result is not motivating. Alfie Kohn writes, "When individuals are threatened with the deprivation of money, status, autonomy, or something else they value, any temporary effect in the desired direction—desired, that is, by the individual with the power to issue these threats—is usually more than offset by the demoralization that occurs." (p.22). That is, these high-stakes tests do more harm than good.

Norm-referenced tests (NRT) are a fraud perpetrated on the unsuspecting public; they are a fraud because they claim to give information that is valuable about student performance, when in fact NRTs scores are always given in percentiles. They report unfair comparisons of the group that took the test; half are above the median (middle) score and half are below. But one must remember that any group can be described by a bell curve, even if the group is composed of successful students or business people. It is the very nature of the bell curve to rank people against each other. The fact remains that any group will produce scores that range in a bell-shaped curve: that is, 10 percent at the top and bottom, 20 percent at the next level of the top and bottom, and 40 percent in the middle. The average score (mean) is a more telling score in that it more accurately represents the group taking the test. Such tests as the Iowa Test of Basic Skills (ITBS) are recalibrated every seven years; that is, the mean score is placed at the middle of the group (50th percentile). So, even as the mean score rises as students get better, the test scoring is recalibrated to keep the bell curve shape. The achievement gains of the students over the seven years are wiped out by such a process. (see: Berliner & Biddle, 1995).

Teachers have little or no control over the factors that influence their students' scores on standardized tests. Yet, they are held accountable for these scores; this is a fraud perpetuated by various testing systems and supported by state funds. Low scores on achievement tests are most often associated with low social and economic factors; in others words, by class, race and gender—the very characteristics the students brought with them when they entered the classroom. Furthermore, the tests are not accurate enough to give consistent and reliable results over time. The variance of performance by students can be as high as 10 percent on retesting. If rewards and punishments are based on a student's scores, they are hardly reliable indices to make any kind of fair distribution of bonuses or punishments.

The education columnist Michael Winerip (NY Times, 5/7/03) reported that data reported by Paul E. Peterson, a Harvard School of Education professor, had left out a significant number of black students in his study of the voucher system supported so strongly by George W. Bush in 2000. At the time, reporters such as William Safire and Jim Lehrer had quoted Peterson as providing evidence that the voucher system worked. *The Boston Herald* (Aug. 30, 2000) wrote: "The facts are clear and persuasive: school vouchers work..." Winerip tells us that a Princeton professor, Alan B. Krueger, restudied the very same data and after two years reports that Professor Peterson had it all wrong. By analyzing the data, Krueger found that as many as 292 students should have been labeled as blacks but had been eliminated out of the final count. That raised the number of blacks in the sample studied to 811 instead of 519. The recalculation of the study means that "the impact of a voucher offer is not statistically significant." Others have reviewed Krueger's review of Peterson's study and concluded in support of Krueger's findings. For the very least, Peterson's work was not the stuff on which one should be making policy decisions. But, of course, that is the way it works. Politics is always in play when educational research is published. We always have to rely on creating an open-door policy for the review and evaluation of even the research designed to evaluate. Everything is in question; all must be debated if we are going to have even a small chance for finding sense and meaning in what is going on.

The claim is made that high stakes testing has improved students' math scores. Imagine this statement being true. How did these tests do it? Is it the tests themselves? Is it incentives versus punishments that move the teachers who, in turn, move students to do better on mathematics tests? Are teachers finally deciding that they had better work harder and more effectively in the teaching of mathematics? Are students seeing now that their teachers really care about how well they do on the math tests, so they are working harder to do better on the tests? A press report (*NY Times*, Apr. 23, 2003) regarding a Stanford University study shows that when tests are linked with consequences, eighth-grade black students' competency rates increased by 3.65 percent, while Hispanic students' rates increased by 4.06 percent. Even more impressive, it reports that "national math scores between 1996 and 2000 rose an average of seven-tenths of one percent in states with no consequences, 1.2 percent in those states that simply published the results in the newspaper and 1.6 percent in states that either rewarded success or penalized failure." (Winter, 2003)

One would think such information would close the debate, but no, that is not the case. The above gains are relatively small in an environment that is very complicated with multiple factors contributing to outcomes. Even when one acknowledges the gains as real, even impressive given that math scores have not moved much over the last decade, it is a giant leap to credit the tests with consequences as the cause of the gains. Robert L. Linn, a former president of the American Educational Research Association, has been quoted as saying, "To be able to definitely attribute results to the stakes of a test is a stretch for any of them." (Ibid.) After all is said and done, the teachers themselves, when polled, overwhelmingly agree that high-stakes testing contradicts their own ideas of sound educational practice.

The news from Britain is that Education Secretary, Charles Clark, has announced the postponement of national test results for two years while the tests are honed and geared to teachers' assessments of student achievement. The previous education secretary, Estelle Morris, resigned when schools missed the national achievement target scores and protests by teachers and parents were raised. Mr. Clark says that testing is an important "way of finding at an early stage where improvements needed to be made." He wants a more relaxed testing regime with more emphasis on teachers' assessment. What he has discovered is precisely what Robert Linn has recommended to policymakers in the United States: namely, to refrain from putting all one's weight on a single test and then using that test to make important decisions. Rather, Linn recommends that educators use multiple indicators of performance. Linn also recommends that tests should be built on previously constructed standards and that these standards should be set high, but realistically attainable. (Linn, 1998)

We have focused on the issue of high-stakes testing for two reasons: first, it is a current debate about how to improve schools through accountability, and second, high-stakes testing is closely related to a package notion of knowledge and its acquisition. The belief about knowledge as a package possessed by some and not by others is deeply held in American culture. It runs parallel with the other deeply held American belief, namely that one's children are all above average in the ways it counts. In other words, people seem to believe that knowledge is not real and useful unless it is capable of be held in secret by some people and denied access to others. The concept of an "elite education" is congruent with the belief in knowledge understood as a package versus understanding knowledge as the processing of experience.

High-stakes testing is committed to the idea of knowledge as a package that can be sorted by pieces and graded true and false. Only so, can one assume that a multiple-choice test has any validity, as what is tested must be understood as stable and unchanging across cultures. An open society, on the other hand, must admit to many interpretations of human experience, not a single unchanging body of knowledge. Pericles' famous funeral oration praises Athens against Sparta as, "Our city is thrown open to the world..." It was not a closed society and, therefore, its citizens were free to explore and express their ideas. "We are free to live exactly as we please," Pericles said. An open society does not have private banks of knowledge locked away preventing access by the "unworthy." At the end of his eulogy on Athens, Pericles said, "I claim that Athens is the School of Hellas, and that the individual Athenian grows up to develop a happy versatility, a readiness for emergencies, and self-reliance." (Popper, 1945) The open society holds onto a faith in reason and humanitarian instincts. This is not to say that Athens was perfect, but for its time, it left a model of democracy and a vision of what human beings may reach for in self-governance.

In the postmodern world we find these traditional statements in support of freedom of thought consistent with the emergence of knowledge and understanding as a work in process. Umberto Eco in his book, *The Open Work,* proposes that art, for example, always leaves some of the meaning of arrangement, design, form, and so forth, open to the public, or merely to chance interpretations, thus making a work of art not a single, closed piece, but made of multiple pieces. If this is so, how do standardized tests come up with "one right answer?" The belief in an elite view of knowledge embraces a closed, single, inner meaning available only to a few. Peter Brook, on the other hand, tells us in *The Open Door* that there are no magic formulas to success in the artistic process. This does not mean there is not such a thing as quality work involving:"...questions of visibility, pace, clarity, articulation, energy, musicality, variety, rhythm...all these need to be observed, in a strictly practical and professional way." *(Brook, 1995, p. 144)*

Secrets are the essences of Platonic philosophy, of private societies, of so-called privileged groups. But, Brook would tell us to wake up! The surprise is there is no surprise! There are no secrets! Knowledge is the ongoing ever-changing making of sense about human experience. This makes it very nearly impossible to create meaningful standardized tests for a national audience. The advocates of high stakes testing are committed to believing in the management of society on a very large scale. This once was called utopia. And there is a strange quality of utopians that they are willing to sacrifice the few in order to serve the many and they think the have the secret knowledge of how to do it. Karl Popper (1944) rebuts some of the practical repercussions of the myth of utopian progress, in particular the holistic fallacy that the management of society can be done only on the grand scale. He argues that it is the whole of society that we must endeavor to reshape. Against this he proposes that the main business of social engineering must be the elimination of specific sources of misery. Popper defines the acquiring knowledge as a process of trial and error: "We make progress if and only if," Popper writes, "we are prepared to learn from our mistakes: to recognize our errors and to utilize them critically instead of persevering in them dogmatically. (pp. 314).

Marginalized students are also diverse students who have been miss-educated as if there is a world of privileged, private knowledge from which they are denied access by the very fact of their failure on standardized tests. Carlos Cortes, in his book, *The Children Are Watching,* believes that privilege is the force undermining the very fabric of our society. In particular, the media are constantly sending damaging messages to marginalized students.

Traditional politics is like traditional teaching; they both embrace the notion that convictions should be "received" from authority rather than constructed personally by experience. The danger of traditional teaching is the prospect of a totalitarian educational outcome. This may sound extreme, but critical thinking skills are a treat to traditional teachers who would not instill convictions, but rather destroy the capacity to form any convictions. John Taylor Gratto was the "teacher of the year" in New York State in 1991. He spent the year visiting schools and making speeches and ended up writing a book about his experiences, *Dumbing Us Down* (2002). He found that teaching means different things in different places, but that there is a "hidden curriculum in compulsory schooling," common to most school districts. Gratto is pessimistic about the possibility of schools breaking out of a pattern of confusion, indifference, emotional dependence and student labeling. As a result students have no personal power or space in most schools (pp. 2-10).

Gratto's hidden curriculum helps understand why it is that principals insist that the first order of business expected from teachers is that they develop *control* over their classroom. The most stunning criticism that an administrator can apply to a teacher is: "She does not have control over her students." It is not merely because principals want a nice quiet school where everyone is quietly working to fill out their workbooks, rather it is the deeper control of the individual students in some order of group think. When politicians and school administrators speak of raising standards in schools, what they mean is eliminating the annoying failures of marginalized students. The main strategy for doing so is to eliminate remedial courses as a way of keeping out those who do not think like one should in the mainstream.

We use the term "marginalized" to describe students who are ignored, whether for poverty, race, ethnicity, or gender; Gratto (2000) uses the term "dumb." He says that teachers call students they do not like, "dumb." In effect, teachers wish the "dumb" into existence. "…[T]hey serve valuable functions: as a danger to themselves and others, they have to be watched, classified, disciplined, trained, medicated, sterilized, ghettoized, cajoled, coerced, jailed." (p. xxxi) Once a major portion of the school population is so labeled "dumb," then they may be treated, "for their own good," differently from the rest of the students. Gratto quotes Woodrow Wilson who saw the education issue a class problem: "We want one class to have a liberal education. We want another class, a very much larger class of necessity, to forego the privilege of a liberal education and fit themselves to perform specific difficult manual tasks." (p. 38) How far have we come since Woodrow Wilson's casual assumption that the great majority of the American school population was only fit for "manual tasks?" In contemporary America, most of the manual tasks in manufacturing and industry are shipped overseas. There are no manual tasks left, except minimum-wage, part-time work in fast food, or on farms and lawn care in the suburbs. For example, Delta Airlines has contracted out its reservation and information system to India. In India thousands of college graduate workers answer Delta Airways phones in perfect English for the sum of $200 per month. And people ask for the reasons of American unemployment! Imagine living on $200 a month in America, much less asking a college graduate to be happy to settle for such a salary!

What has happened to the public schools in America is the segregation between the elites and the marginalized in an environment of passivity. Creating a generation or two of passive students with limited job opportunities, even if one has a college degree, has created a population that is dependent on national leaders who are committed only to their own agenda. A dependent population does not rebel, so the hierarchy of leaders can feel safe with workers and the unemployed. The results are a massive resegregation of classes, races, gender and ethnic differences. The schism of resegregation breaks down into smaller groups of angry people who are no threat to the elected hierarchy and their mouthpieces—the public news media that controls what gets said and heard. Gratto writes that "in the space of one lifetime, the United States was converted from a place where human variety had ample room to display itself into a laboratory of virtual orthodoxy—a process concealed by dogged survival of the mythology of independence." (2000, p. 121).

The E.M.Kauffman Foundation of Kansas City has made an investment in the improvement of city schools; in particular, they have provided financial support for minority students who want to go to college. Mr. Kauffman, personally, was committed to helping poor and minority students from his own high school, Westport High, in Kansas City, get a college education. (Winerip, April 23, 2003) He targeted ninth-grade students by offering them a free college education if they were drug-free, not pregnant, and had graduated from Westport High. Over the first years of the program, he expanded this offer to include several of the Kansas City high schools. The numbers created by this generous offer are not encouraging. One thousand three hundred and ninety-four students participated. Of these 1,394 students, 767 graduated from high school, or 56 percent of the participants. Of these high-school graduates, only 16 percent earned a bachelor's degree and another six percent received a vocational degree in community colleges. As the program discovered, the Foundation did not know how far behind these students were by the time they reached the ninth grade. Since then, the Foundation and the school system have collaborated in a community-based program and modified the amount of funding each participant receives. Michael Winerip of *The New York Times* reported that, "Kauffman officials learned that the promise of a college degree was too abstract." The program has since become more intensive beginning in middle school and following through with support and mentoring throughout their secondary education. The participants now have a summer program in their junior and senior years at Kansas State University. The program seeks to create partnerships with other colleges and universities to improve students' performance in the basics and influence students to stay in school and stay focused on educational achievement.

The Kansas City experience, with the best of intentions on the part of the Kauffman Foundation, illustrates that money is not enough motivation or incentive to promote academic success in marginalized students. More and more, educational reform researchers are finding it necessary to engage with communities' political processes in order to move educational reform and produce permanent improvements. There is a fierce battle going on for the leadership of educational reform and, make no mistake, the battleground is political and ideological. Schooling is embedded in ideological conflicts over control of what is taught, who receives attention, who goes on to higher education and, therefore, who goes on to win decent jobs in a narrowing job market economy. See Zeus Leonardo's review of two new books on the political and social issues in public school reform: *Education and Democratic Theory: Finding a Place for Community Participation in Public School Reform* by A. Belden Fields and Walter Feinberg; and *The Color of School Reform: Race, Politics and the Challenge of Urban Education,* by Henig, Hula, Orr, and Pedescleaux. Race and class relations seem to be best understood when studied together because of their mutual dependency. Race, some would argue, is the primary and maybe the crucial issue in understanding the difficulty in effecting school reform. Leonardo argues that though race may be given "a privileged place, even a dominate one...[i]t must be understood in the context of other social and ideological systems." (p. 38) He reminds us that educational reform research cannot focus on one factor without the other. "Because race and class oppression are reinforcing systems, educational research must explain their symbiotic relationship in order to provide radical alternatives." (Ibid.)

In *The Color of School Reform,* Henig, et al., report on their research on four black urban cities' schools: Washington, D.C. (95 percent black children by the 1970s), Detroit, Atlanta, and Baltimore. All of these cities struggle to maintain academic quality. The students in these school communities face tremendous challenges learning to read, write and perform mathematical calculations to the level of higher education admission. The problem is so huge that these researchers regard the urban centers of America as "ghettos." The white flight from urban centers after the Brown decision left the schools of America's major cities to black leadership and the physical and material resources of schooling in poor to miserable conditions. School violence was increasingly a serious problem turning high schools into prison-like fortresses with security guards and metal detectors and body searches at each entrance. After centuries of white dominance of public schools, these urban schools must construct coalitions of community support if meaningful school reform is to happen. Leonardo quotes Henig's statement on developing civic capacity and it deserves repeating here: "There is no way around politics. To the contrary, the concept of civic capacity, which lies at the core of our framework, suggests that the prospect for meaningful and sustainable reform depends upon lines of conflict and cooperation among a wide array of actors, both inside and outside the educational arena." *(p. 9).*

This challenge is easier to state than to meet with effective actions. White leaders are fearful of being labeled colonialists. Black leaders are afraid of being called "Uncle Toms" if they even talk to white businessmen. The Detroit Compact was understood by many blacks as a form of "plantation politics." And castigations of "Oreo" attributions are feared yet rendered frequently within the urban community. So the prospects of building civic capacity to meet the needs of urban school reform are thin indeed. The temptations to cynicism again lay a claim upon us; and we must exercise our hope that positive social change can happen and that students can benefit from improved school conditions.

Marginalized students are not limited to African-American in urban schools. There are Native-Americans, Hispanic-Americans, Asian-Americans, and rural, poor Americans. The pursuit of justice and fair play in the school curriculum regarding the issue of linguistic diversity in multicultural classrooms is of particular difficulty. Currently, there is an upsurge of conservative political pressure to support "English-only" curriculum programs and end bilingual programs.

Bilingual programs are not merely about a second language; they are about maintaining connectivity with the culture of the second language. Often when students are encouraged to speak only English, they feel disconnected and disenfranchised from their family culture. Hispanic students, for example, would feel that a Latino culture was second-class compared with the English language culture. When they feel their culture is second-class, they also feel they are personally second-class students. This seems to be true with all second language students. Rather than being recognized as fluent in two languages of equal value, English as a Second Language students feels ridiculed for possessing a native language other than English. (Nieto, 1992, p. 157) Some educators and political leaders suggest that immersion is English language is the way to the quickest entry into full-time English language instruction. The problem with this strategy is that it perpetuates the second class citizenship aura surrounding the native language of minorities. Nieto reports how a seventh-grade Navajo student felt about learning and maintaining his Native-American language: "The ability to communicate in two languages is an advantage because I can talk and understand my elders...[B]eing bilingual is also important for maintaining the native tongue. Without this, our language will die out. This cannot happen because it is the basis of our culture." (p. 161) For reasons like these, Nieto supports the use of long-term language maintenance programs, as the second language facility provides access to and identity with the native culture. (Ibid.) So, there are emotional developmental reasons for supporting long-term bilingual programs.

Even though there are many advantages to the students in bilingual programs there are problems in maintaining them in public schools. First, they are expensive. Second, teachers feel the support of second language development undercuts their instructional authority in English language curricula. Third, the teaching materials in the second language are often literal translations of English cultural materials that have little meaning for the native language culture. There is no such thing as one to one language substitution when translating educational materials. Finally, when badly executed bilingual curricula fail the students in the program are blamed for the failure. And, once again, we find the minority student marginalized. Because many bilingual programs are designed to self-destruct by phasing out and guiding students into mainstream English culture curricula, the students feel that a part of their own identity is expected to be phased out.

Behind the bilingual education debate one finds a deeply rooted commitment on the part of a sizeable majority of the American population to single cultural ideals. Multiculturalism is often attacked as "anti-American," therefore, unpatriotic. Foreign languages in general are suspect by the "Speak American, boy, so I can understand" crowd. European immigrant families are often proud of mastering American English quickly and easily. They tend to adopt majority styles in clothing and goods, opting not to be different. So, they and their current ancestors are committed strongly to sameness in language and style. They, therefore, communicate to minority populations that second languages and minority cultural symbolism are "not as good" as mainstream America. This attitude is difficult to explain and support on ideological grounds alone, especially if one examines the huge multilingual and multicultural contributions that all kinds of immigrants have made to the American melting pot. Those who do acknowledge the melting pot notion of the creation of American life, often mean by this idea a support of a single new amalgamation for American culture. Rather than enjoying and relishing one's native language and culture, within the context of living in the United States, the popular notion often ridicules diversity in language and style.

A curricular reform of major dimensions needs to be accomplished if public schools are to include within the K-12 educational design a commitment to diversity and its positive value in American life. Fostering assimilation of differences into a single melting pot, no longer works, if it ever did. The teaching of tolerance and respect for diversity is not common in American classrooms, if it were to mean equity for African-Americans, Hispanics, Native-Americans, Asians (of all types), or if it were to mean equity and valuation for religious diversity in beliefs and practices, or if it were to mean equity for gender differences and sexual orientations. The public school curricula have a long way to go to meet these objectives. In the meantime, we are faced with the obligation to address the needs of marginalized students currently in the school and college systems.

Joan Kernan Cone teaches English in a California high school and writes about her experiences teaching an integrated (non-tracked) journalism class to seniors. (Cone, 2003). She found her class divided between those who were academically successful and academic failures. She raises questions as to how this division happens within the walls of the school. Even as the high school was attempting to detrack curricular enrollments, the high school counselors used math and science experience as the deciding factors in assigning classes. For example, students who were put in the Algebra A class were taught by teachers who had little control over the classes and did not explain the math concepts very well. Cone is convinced that the placement of students in the initial math class, "set in motion choices of subsequent courses through the rest of high school" (p. 5). Thus, these students built their academic identities around low achievement: they cut classes, acted out resentment, did little class work or homework. In turn, the students who saw themselves as low achievers, convinced their teachers that they were not worthy of teacher attention. So, the teacher expectations and the low achieving students' negative behaviors were self-reinforcing. On the basis of her study, Cone suspects that programming decisions by school counselors exercised powerful influence on the high-school careers of students by virtue of their race and class. And she concludes that teachers and the school collude in carefully constructing the conditions for success or failure of their students.

We find these secondary school programming decisions continue to carry on their influence on students' self-appraisal in higher education. Entering college and university academics, such marginalized students expect failure and second-class treatment. But if diverse student mixes can be maintained in classes and lab groups, students can change their self-appraisals as they find success working with other successful students. One of our teacher education candidates was amazed when assigned to work on a collaborative team that he not only could do the work, but was leading the team getting the project done on time. Just a small amount of success can change a student's self-assessment into positive terms. Multicultural and integrated classrooms and curricular assignments do work to improve relations among students and personal self-regard. Furthermore, the college instructors in our programs found the integrated and collaborative teams to be more interesting to work with than as single students situated in a competitive classroom environment.

We might as well learn now how to be multicultural and integrated, because the demography of America will change significantly in the next 40 to 50 years. By 2020, over 20 percent of the population will be over 65; but while the elderly population will be predominantly white, the school age population will be largely Hispanic, Asian, African-American and other immigrant peoples. This will be especially true the in large cities of America. (Hodgkinson, 2003) What all this will mean remains to be seen. However, we know that as the percentage of the population over 65 grows, so the support of per-pupil spending by schools reduces. Making a prediction that fiscal crises in education are coming in the next 20 years would seem a reasonable proposition. Reinforcing the likelihood of fiscal crises facing schools is the probability that financial strain due to increases in the social healthcare system for the elderly will be competing for public support with the needs of schools. Inside the schools a multiracial population of students will emerge as racial identity will blur. Hispanics and Asians will constitute 61 percent of the school-age population by 2025. As the white population continues its trend of lower fertility rates, failing to replace their number in the population, the Hispanic, Asian, and African-American populations, will increase by both higher fertility rates, and higher immigration rates. These realities support predictions about language diversity increasing even more than is the case at the beginning of the millennium. Multilingual curricula will be needed to meet the challenge of many second native languages spoken by public school students. School reform will not be an option in the coming 20 years; rather, it will be a necessity (Ibid.).

If a majority of the school population is non-white in the very near future, the neglect of minority relevant curricular materials; the emphasis on English-only instruction; and the degradation of people of color will produce its own calls for reform. College and university recruiting in the next 20 years will also have to change. The services needed to support a more diverse academic population will have to be provided. But if the economic trend toward a wider division in America between the rich and the poor continues while the proportionate number of the poor population grows, then the temptation will be very strong for universities to pursue the rich students and ignore the poor. Currently, there is little evidence that institutions of higher education are embracing their social responsibility for helping to improve public schools. It is costly to recruit poor students from poor neighborhoods, with poor records; costly in time, money and effort on the part of colleges and universities. Our prediction is that not many colleges will undertake such initiatives. In fact, what we see now is the pressure on higher education to raise money from foundations, alumni, government agencies, and wealthy companies. Money-raising is a huge effort in higher education; even the smallest of colleges have a staff focused on fundraising. It would seem to be against the universities' self-interest to recruit students from among the poor segment of the population who will drain fiscal resources, when the more wealthy students bring their own resources to the campus. Of course, there is a moral crisis to all this pursuit of money. As universities keep focused on raising money, they are also teaching their students by example what the university leadership thinks is important. So, we seem to be building a new wealth-oriented culture in America; a wealth-seeking, wealth-inducing, wealth-embracing but not wealth-sharing culture.

There once was a time when even among elite families of America, service toward the common cause and body politic was an accepted norm. Service to public charities and foundations were highly praised as valuable. Lawyers donated a considerable portion of their time to public service, including political office. Medical doctors would give so many days a week to serving the poor and needy; some would even take years off to offer medical services nationally and internationally. Banks have always encouraged their employees to donate a portion of their personal time to serving on boards of public and non-profit agencies. On and on the list could go in praise of public service; but things seem to be changing now, in the direction of privatism.

A major factor in the money crisis in education is the money crisis in the federal budget. The imbalance of payments makes for deep debts; but the country seems committed to foreign intrigue, wars, and buying off allies; while equally committed to spending income on costly foreign goods. In the midst of this economic drift there remains the social commitment to paying our CEOs, athletes, and international consultants extremely high salaries and bonuses. We find it difficult to explain why there is a state fiscal crisis in both Florida and Michigan (and in many other states, as well) that requires schools, colleges, libraries, hospitals, and elderly services to trim their budgets between 3 and 6.5 percent. The difficulty is not in understanding that the federal leadership has spent billions of U.S. dollars on war and foreign commitments, but in explaining to ourselves, colleagues and children why we have chosen to spend less on those very services about which we care the most. This country has the resources to eliminate poverty, build affordable housing, educate the entire citizenry, and care for the aged. But, maybe we do not have the fiscal resources if we are going to perpetrate fraud in our major industries and sponsor soporific sports and entertainment distractions from the work there is yet to be done. We may have cleared the forests, we may have built huge cities, we may have become the most powerful nation in the world, but until we feed the hungry, house the homeless, clothe the naked and educate all our citizens to the same high standards now afforded to only a few, we do not deserve to rest and say "a job well done!"

Deborah Meier (2000) describes her vision of schools for the 21st century as rich and vibrant, communities "that will help to nurture the two indispensable traits of a democratic society: a high degree of tolerance for others, indeed genuine empathy for them, as well as a high degree of tolerance for uncertainty, ambiguity, and puzzlement, indeed enjoyment of them" (p. 30). Meier continues to be committed to the smaller sized school rather than the big schools. She thinks a school of around 400 students is about right. In a small school everyone knows everybody's name, so there is no anonymity behind which to hide. Instead of factory-like schools which marked the 20th century and can be characterized as a world of trained mindlessness, Meier would envision small schools in which "we can...substantially affect the gap between the rich and the poor where it will count" (p. 31).

In the following chapters, we will address the issues of learning, collaboration, access and community building that characterize our vision of democratic schools and our commitment to educational achievement for all. To make this journey we will need to have supportive and experienced companions, like Deborah Meier, to help us keep to our task and our hearts filled with hope for the future.

Issues and Questions for Chapter Three

National testing tends to invite teachers to teaching for the test.

- Education tends to become training and credentialing when schools focus on students passing a test versus understanding an idea.
- How can anyone claim that NCLB is building a national meritocracy, when there is no common curriculum across America?
- Testing is not a form of teaching the content tested. It is a form of teaching fear of schools.
- Why are veteran teachers leaving the profession because of high stakes testing?

High Schools and Colleges Organized around "Successful Students"

- Compare the difference between elite students and marginal students as they apply to college.
- Case studies demonstrate the difference of class among groups of students.
- Why do elite students have preferences, while marginal students struggle with choices?
- Contrast the physical evidence of privilege versus marginal students entering college.

The open society versus the closed society as constructed in schools:

- The concept of "elite education" is congruent with knowledge understood as a package versus knowledge as the processing of experience.

- How can school curricula treat the emergence of knowledge and understanding as a work in process, rather than as a product?
- Marginalized students are also diverse students who have been miss-educated, as if there is a world of private knowledge from which they are denied by the very fact of their failure.
- The media sends out messages of privilege to marginal students and will eventually undermine the very fabric of our society.

Isolation and Loneliness for those on the Margins

- The sense of isolation and of not belonging can lead to self-loathing on the part of victims. This is the other side of the coin of "blaming the victim."
- Yesterday's politics won't work in creating new and just institutions.
- Changing how colleges and high schools treat marginalized students, must also mean changing how they treat all students.
- Many faculty members see themselves as gate-keepers not as access providers.
- Totalitarian education does not instill convictions, but rather destroys the capacity to form any.

"... a teacher expects to learn
From her students.
She yields to their force.
She sees with their eyes.
She is saved from conspiracy
And lives in community."
No. 52 *The Tao of Teaching*

CHAPTER FOUR
Schools as Learning Communities

Schools are communities where both intended and unintended learning occur. Schools are not necessarily buildings, although comfortable, well-equipped buildings are nice. Nor are schools a collection of classrooms. Schools are where teachers and students learn together, focused on a curriculum. There have been schools in the out-of-doors and in cathedrals or mosques. The first universities in the western world were attached to mosques and students sat on the floor while the teacher sat on a bench or chair, usually beside a large column. One can see that arrangement still used in modern-day Cairo. Go to the great old mosque El-Azhar and see the Islam students sitting on rugs on the polished floors and listening to the scholar who leans against the pillar and speaks in the fine Arabic of the Koran and its interpretation. The curriculum is ancient, as well, and includes Arabic grammar, Islamic law, logic, and mathematics, including algebra. These schools spread throughout the Mediterranean world and formed the foundations of western education. Arabic became the common language from Spain to Baghdad, replacing Latin. Of course, the community of learning did change over time and the cathedrals of Europe started to replace the mosques of Islam, at least, on the northern side of the Mediterranean Sea.

The dialogue between teachers and students was the crux of the work to be done in the schools. The emphasis on communication between teacher and student has remained the same, except the content of the dialogue has changed radically, especially since the invention of moveable type and the printing press made books inexpensive enough to be shared by many. But, basically, the conversation of teachers and students has served the educative process from the beginning. The interpretation of a standard religious text was the business of the dialogue, but that expanded over time to interpret human experience of the entire world. So, from the beginning, what was talked about has been the sense we can make of our experiences, including our reading of text. Making sense was the issue in learning to read; literacy was the tool of sense-making and sharing. By "making sense" we mean a mindful engagement with the details of living. Ellen Langer (1997) has written a beautiful book about the power of learning and declares a principle of learning psychology when she writes: "the way information is learned will determine how, why, and when it is used (p.3)." She calls such learning "mindful," because it is self-consciously aware of the determinants of learning. In other words, the context of learning holds the key to unlocking what we may be capable of doing with what is learned. Langer sums up a mindful approach to learning as having "three characteristics: the continuous creation of new categories; openness to new information; and an implicit awareness of more than one perspective (p. 4)." If we apply these characteristics to a school, then the learning that goes on in a mindful school is not tied to one point of view, nor closed to new information, nor inclined to automatic, machine-like behavior.

There is nothing wrong with a teacher lecturing to her students, unless lecturing is the only strategy. Many lectures can excite the silent dialogue that is invited when exciting ideas are presented with a flare. Students will react, both silently and often verbally, sometimes with applause. So, lecturing can be an efficient way to present information and engage students in dialogue. But, most of the time lecturing becomes telling students what to think, how to think, and why to think. We call this type of lecturing, "talking at students." The consequence of talking at students is to create a top-down approach to teaching. It communicates that the teacher is the one in charge and what she says is the official way to understand the world around us. Of course, many times that is the case; the teacher does know what she is talking about and students gain from her shared interpretation of experiences. But, traditional talk-down to the students' approaches tends to confine instruction into an authoritarian mode and has the effect of closing off multiple interpretations of experience. If we are closed to alternative explanations, we are apt to miss other possibilities, including new ideas and creative solutions to difficult problems. Also, openness leads students to interpret for themselves what they are experiencing. This is called thinking and it is why Langer calls her explanation of effective learning "mindful."

When students are encouraged to take charge of their own learning, marvelous things can happen. Deborah Meier (1995) believes that Central Park East was such a success precisely because the students were encouraged to explore multiple ways of understanding and expressing the world around them.

The principal means of student evaluations in Meier's small Harlem school was portfolio presentations. Periodically, the entire school would hold student presentations of their work. Their parents were invited and the teachers and students got to see and hear about the students' work. There was no hiding away a D- paper in the back of a file. Students pasted up on newsprint their accomplishments, their attempts, and in so doing they shared their dreams and pride. This approach to learning acknowledges that students and teachers are human and humans basically like to talk. So, they create groups for talking, sharing, checking out their ideas, and testing their relationships. This is community; the particularly human domain of social interaction.

Steven Pinker (2002) quotes Eric Hoffer, the longshoreman and philosopher, about the human community instinct. "When people are free to do as they please, they usually imitate each other (p. 63)." Aping others is a very human characteristic and explains why we feel more comfortable in a community where we can see, talk, and imitate each other. Also, being with others offers one multiple sources of information all at once. We can learn what works and what does not work for others, before we try out the idea ourselves. And what we learn most decidedly is learned from our peers. We watch others our own age and measure ourselves against their behavior. In adults we call this instinct "style," and in children we call it "peer pressure."

School learning is always social, communal and engaged. North Central Regional Educational Laboratory (NCREL) reports a strong consensus among researchers of the importance of what they call "engaged learning." What engaged learning means is that students need to be focused on the curriculum in a community setting. What is valued by Jones, Valez, Nowakowski, and Rasmussen (1994) are learners who are excited by problem-solving and able to transfer knowledge from one context to another. From the beginning years of schooling, they argue a reformed educational system would foster collaboration among learners and the capacity to work together creatively. Lee Shulman (1999) encourages teachers "to support learners in the active, collaborative, reflective reexamination of ideas in a social context (p.12)." Shulman favors describing the learning context as a learning community because he believes knowledge is more useful when it is public and communal, rather than private and hidden. Indeed, learning is more useful when shared in community. When instruction and evaluation is disconnected from the communal context, that is, when the focus is on the isolated individual competing against everyone else, learning activities become tools of control and often end with a sense of failure.

Since we now know that learning occurs in specific contexts and is always connected to the original context of the learning, the learner's sense of failure in schools that isolate and marginalize him/her remains connected to school. Bruner (1996) argued in his book, *The Culture of Education*, that not only what we think, but how we think is linked to the cultural context of the learning going on. We learn in context by learning from others and ourselves, who we are and who we are becoming. So learning in community connects the past with the creation of the new world emerging. Students, after all, are not clones of their parents; they are adapting, changing, creating and fixing a new transformative situation. In order for students to construct a transformed environment, the need to be engaged with what is happening in their classroom community. In other words, they need to "be there," rather than only half present.

Engaged learning does not mean "trying harder," if the trying is merely repetitive. The students at the University

Campus School in Worcester, MA, an experimental school with collaborative commitments with Clark University, work hard and are deeply engaged in their struggles to learn. A *New York Times'* story (Zezima, June 4, 2003) tells of the school's first graduation class of 31 students, all of whom are going to college next fall. Clark University and the Worcester Public School created a rigorous neighborhood high school. Its students were neighborhood residents and not specially picked but recruited by the school staff from the neighborhood. They took in students with little reading skills, immigrant students, students without mathematics skills. The teachers were nothing special either; some were recent graduates from Clark University; others had worked a long time in the Worcester schools. They had the idea that ordinary students and ordinary teachers could be engaged in the learning necessary to apply successfully for college admissions. One student is quoted as saying of his teachers: "If someone puts so much work into you, you don't want to let them down (Ibid.)." While it has not been easy, what has occurred in University Park Campus School is engagement with the world, with books, with science, and public affairs. This small school (200 students) succeeded because teachers and students and parents were engaged with each other and no one wanted "to let anyone down." The principal, Donna Rodrigues, explains the school's success as creating a culture of hard work and the expectations for success. This story beautifully defines what we think engaged learning is all about. In this sense, there are no magic secrets to school success. Schools succeed when the hard work of learning is offered with respect for the community of learners, both teachers and students.

Many understand the profession of teaching as performing before an audience. On the other hand, more and more teachers are coming to see their role as convener of a community of learners. Howard Gardner in his book, *The Open Mind,* describes his experiences in China where he observed teaching understood as giving a performance. The Chinese teachers were well trained and performers in the sense that they demanded from their students to imitate the teacher. Gardner, however, encourages a teaching model that convenes rather than guides, coaches rather than demands imitation. Performance implies that the students act as an audience and that learning means copying the master. "Be like me!" While some imitation is always present in learning as students reach out to try on new ideas, students become their own masters through the appropriation process. Ideas become "my ideas." Also, Lynn Paine (1990) confirms Gardner's descriptions of Chinese teaching as a "virtuoso" model. The virtuoso expert model seems to work with the very young students, and, indeed, Chinese schools are very good at the early levels of learning. They cover the basics very well. It is later on, in professional education that the Chinese system seems to be less inspiring. Gardner tells us that "the Chinese are not good at give and take. They are comfortable with reading prepared text but do not like to be asked questions spontaneously and even less happy about fielding impromptu questions (p. 151)."

The point of the comparison with Chinese educational pedagogy is that the way one is taught is how one will think. If students are discouraged from spontaneous exploratory ideas, they will eventually avoid them. If students are expected to repeat facts drilled by the teacher, it is not surprising that students end up forgetting much of the content. We make these observations not to encourage sloppy, unorganized teaching or spontaneous, make-it-up-as-one-goes-along curriculum. Rather, planned and scheduled discussions and engagements with challenging ideas invite students to construct their own explanations for how people and the world works. Permitting, even encouraging, students to make mistakes and learn from them is basic to making progress in understanding (Popper, 1944). Popper calls this kind of progress "piecemeal social engineering," by which he means learning based on experiences one step at a time. One of the clear advantages of Popper's social recipe is that it avoids utopian ambitions and the temptations of hierarchical authoritarianism. Utopian systems always end up sacrificing the individual for the so-called common good, decided by whomever is in charge of the organization.

Students are marginalized in the learning process when they are expected to speak with the teacher's voice rather than with their own voice. Donaldo Macedo writes about the built-in prejudices of what he calls the "White liberal pedagogy (1994)." When white teachers pay lip service, Macedo asserts, to antiracism and social justice, there is an enormous gap between avowed commitments and the social praxis that creates the political actions which challenge oppression and privilege. Macedo follows Paulo Freire's vision of school reform as a historical movement that "affirms men as beings who transcend themselves...Hence it identifies with the movement which engages men as being aware of their incompletion... an historical movement which has its point of departure, its subjects and its objects (1994, p. 182)." Engaged learning is only possible when the learners themselves are as much the subjects as they are objects. Learning is something that happens inside of human beings and to acknowledge that learning is occurring is to identify the learner as a respected subject and object of knowledge. To marginalize students is to withhold the respect students deserve as learners. We communicate disrespect to students when we expect them to fail. We hear teachers say that they teach history or mathematics, but we say that, in fact, they teach students. The discipline knowledge is respected only as it is held and used by a learner, inside them. So, all knowledge learned changes a person. Once a person engages to learn the multiplication tables, for example, that person is committed to never being the same again. Such a student is constructing inside of him/herself a new person who can do things s/he could not to before, and therefore, the student can take pride in being a new person, deserving respect. Learning, therefore, is a product of experience and not the adoption of some ideological abstract.

Dewey taught us to be suspicious of abstractions like "good and evil," not because they do not exist, but because all experience of things good and things evil is concrete. As Dewey wrote, "I don't need an absolute to enable me to distinguish between the good of kindness and the evil of slander, or the good of health, and the evil of valetudinarianism. In experience, things bear their own specific characters (quoted by Westbrook, 1991, p. 143)." Treating school knowledge as definable abstractions that can be tested objectively in individuals is to create a mythical system of sorting human beings on a basis other than human experience. We may not be able to avoid some kind of sorting of students in the educational process, but we can take care to be anti-oppressive about it. Kevin Kumashiro (in Howell & Tuitt, 2003, p. 47) discusses the complexities of avoiding oppressing students with non-inclusive curricula. He refers to Britzman's studies that show students wanting to learn what affirms their identities and values. The difficulty comes when students examine their beliefs and values, they resist changing what they bring to class and so are resistive to disruptive and disaffirming knowledge. Kusmashiro identifies the tendency of learners and teachers to seek out repetitive and familiar stories to explain who they are in relation to others. Once again, we witness the fact that genuine learning means giving up what one thought they knew in order to accommodate the new and connected reality. Learning comes at the price of personal discomfort that challenges ones old absolutes.

If we seek to assist students who are non-privileged in our society, we have to search for ways to avoid marginalizing their efforts and minimizing their accomplishments. One path for exploration of anti-oppressive curricula is to acknowledge that absolutes cannot be the basis of curriculum construction, because we have no way to agree on what to classify as absolute. The Platonic dualism problem reasserts its presence when knowledge is idealized for curricular repetition of past cultural assumptions. There is no way for students to engage deeply in exploring a curriculum that denies their own experience. Absolutist curricula do deny the human experiences of many categories of students, whether they be racial, ethnical, gender-based, or have a spiritual orientation. Curricular commitments to a singular perspective ultimately create divisions, the ins and the outs, the "us and the thems," and, of course, the right versus the wrong.

The problem with absolutes is also related to the problem of using the term "ability." I.Q. tests are supposedly assessing a pre-existent quality that is fixed to a certain degree at the time of birth (conception?). So, it is common for teachers and parents to think about children as having "fixed abilities." In fact, children pick up the jargon of educators and prefer to think of themselves as "smart" rather than "hard-working." There may be some cognitive biological structure that makes some people smarter or more able than other people. But we cannot know this, because every instrument we have to measure intelligence is a cultural construction and not an absolute blueprint of inner cognitive capacities.

Furthermore, Robert Sternberg (1998) reminds us that the traditional model of abilities "may be the cause of rather than a potential answer to educational problems, in particular, and societal problems, in general. The traditional model is part of the problem, not a basis for a solution (p.15-16)." When educators are persuaded of the validity of tests for abilities, they begin to believe in the reality of fixed intelligences that account for student differences. The traditional model of abilities, therefore, induces educators and sometimes parents, as well, to think that student achievement is mostly accounted for by prior existing abilities.

Sternberg argues for a developing-expertise model of intelligence. He writes that "individuals are constantly in a process of developing expertise when they work within a given domain. They may and do, of course, differ in rate and asymptote of development. The main constraint in achieving expertise is not some fixed prior level of capacity, but *purposeful engagement involving direct instruction, active participation, role modeling, and reward*" (pp. 16-17, emphasis added). Engaged learning is the process by which achievements are attained. The planning for engagement to happen in classrooms, calls upon teachers to create community or culture of exploration and excitement in discovery and discourse. Sternberg puts it this way: "The key to developing expertise is purposeful and meaningful engagement in a set of tasks relevant to the development of expertise, something of which any individual is capable of in some degree (p. 18)."

Because individuals differ, they differ absolutely. That is, individuals differ across the entire range of human experience. We inherit from our parents different genes (DNA profiles) and therefore we vary biologically. We also vary culturally by the kind of environmental contexts in which we are raised.

But, what we all have in common and about which there is no variation, is that we all can learn. All human beings have the capacity to develop skills, understanding and construct meaningful explanations of their experiences. Of course, there are differences among students as to how effectively or thoroughly they learn a particular skill or expertise. But, there is not a fixed mental reservoir of individual capacities that will predict outcomes of learning nor account for differences among student achievements.

Engaged learning is radically different from such traditional forms of learning as rote learning, memorization, repetition and group recitals. Ellen Langer is convinced that mindful learning protects future possibilities and leaves one open to the future. She writes, "Information learned in an absolute form can be memorized. It remains still with each repetition, regardless of context and perspective (1997, p. 81)." So, what happens is that rote learning keeps information inflexible and stagnant. Engaged learning allows information to be applied in a variety of contexts. Again, Langer tells us, "If we simply memorize the known past, we are not preparing ourselves for the as-yet-to-be-known future (Ibid.)."

Ellen Langer has studied learning in a variety of settings. Her findings have been supported by a large study headed up by Linda Darling-Hammond and her team of researchers. She and her colleagues studied five experimental high schools in New York City and published the results of the study ("Reinventing High School: Outcomes of the Coalition Campus Schools Project") in the *American Educational Research Journal* (2002).

The study found that the five new schools that were created in New York City replacing a large but failing comprehensive high school "produced, as a group, substantially better attendance, lower incident rates, better performance on reading and writing assignments, higher graduation rates, and higher college-going rates than the previous school, despite serving a more educationally disadvantaged population of students (p. 639)." Her study reports that several factors showed consistent and repeated relationship to school success. Critical are "small size" of the classes and school, an emphasis on personal relationships, a thoughtful curriculum, focus on students developing problem solving skills, and a school wide assessment program *(p. 653)*.

These findings are consistent with the research findings about collaborative and cooperative education approaches for the last 25 years. Strange to say, that after a quarter century of research on learning in collaborative settings, the results have not been more widely accepted by the public. Generally, most people still seem to think that learning is a private and personal matter and that somehow collaboration is cheating or something worse. But, as we have discussed before, healthy adults always choose to work with other humans when they have a choice. So too for high school students

What Darling-Hammond described in her report is the importance of two realities for successful schools: one is *engaged learning* and the second is the power of a *community of learners*. The kind of evaluation explicit in these large end-of-course projects is performance-based assessment of real world tasks. In other words, these students were engaged in authentic tasks that were shared mutually with other students. Frank McCourt (1999) describes how engaging his students with the authentic tasks of interviewing relatives and writing about families may have saved his teaching career in his first year of teaching freshman English in a Staten Island high school. He had found a stack of old essay papers in a closet in his room. He started reading them and found them interesting examples of students struggling to improve their writing. McCourt read some of the essays to his class and discovered that many of the essay writers were parents or relatives of his current students. The students were stunned and emotional about discovering a part of their personal history hiding in this closet.

The papers were so old and brittle that the class was afraid to lose them by disintegration, so McCourt assigned the students in his class the task of copying the essays by hand. Hundreds of these essays were stacked in the classroom closet. In addition to copying over these essays, the students started writing about them, writing about their families. Everyone started coming to class with a pen to write compositions of "My Life." So McCourt discovered engaged learning and the authenticity of the essays made teaching fun and possible for him. He describes his insight into authentic teaching, as beginning when he decided to give up the curriculum that was handed to him and "begin enjoying the act of teaching". (1999 p. 340). McCourt also discovered another characteristic of successful classroom teaching, namely the teacher as co-learner with the students. Recasting the stack of hundreds of essays into the stories of family lives was a classroom-wide discovery. McCourt was a participant in the exciting learning that was going on along with his students. Both teacher and students were engaged in a real project and both found what they were learning interesting and special to each one personally and to the class collectively.

This was our experience in Michigan, also. In Southfield, an English/Language Arts teacher in a middle school invited her students to write family histories or biographies. This writing assignment turned out to be an annual event with incredible community impact because some of the parents could not read while others couldn't speak English. The writing assignment improved home language acquisition; some parents started learning to read and speak English. In Marquette, students wrote cultural histories including, histories of the mining industry and economy and found they had profound ownership in these histories.

McCourt's class felt more like a special community once the project of family essays got started. There was the excitement of feeling that they, both students and teacher, were discovering something together. They felt what they were doing was unique. It was "theirs." The class ownership of the project transformed them into a community of special purpose. This is why the researchers on learning emphasize the context of engagement as extremely important to the learners. Once the project was mutually defined, the class could set goals for itself, have conversations about the meaning of what they were doing, both with each other and with the adults in their lives outside of the classroom. Families contributed to the process by responding to interviews about the relatives who wrote those generation-old essays. In this way, the students' work was viewed as meaningful in the broader world beyond the classroom itself.

The engaged student is learning by transfer from one context to another. Instruction that engages students plans for crossings of context is part of the instructional design. Students acquire ideas by testing them in a variety of contexts. Analysis of ideas is experiencing and expressing ideas in different ways and so it is the very opposite of rote learning of a list of items considered important by the teacher or parent or someone in authority. Lists are useful for filing away, storing, but not necessarily for learning. In other words, the form of action in teaching must be congruent with the substance of the ideas being analyzed. Engagement feeds on finding congruency in experience. When a student grasps an idea, the first thing s/he wants to do is to find a new context in which to apply it or use it in a new way. This explains why high-stakes testing is, in fact, detrimental to learning. To memorize lists and store facts for a specified test of achievement is to prepare to discard such information after the taking of the test.

Engaged learning, Dewey (1910) understood, was an adventure in thinking about experience. Thinking is how humans mediate between themselves and the world around them. Thought transforms the specific to abstract and from abstract to specific. Wisdom learned is the capacity to generalize from experience and test the consequences of our ideas in practice. Good and beneficial results of practical action can then reinforce an idea as useful. Once this meaningful cycle of experience, reflection, and generalization to application in new contexts is acquired by a student, what is learned is clearly his/her own intellectual property, so to speak. The consistency of our ideas tested in experience is what philosophers mean by logic. Knowledge about the world consists of applying logic in various contexts. When students experience the power of their own ideas they do so with grief at having to give up false or unproven ideas and values. So, there is a bittersweet emotion to learning new ideas about the world, as the old and preconceived notions are given up in favor of new ideas that prove they are useful.

What students learn from their acquisition of new ideas about themselves and the world is that both they as individuals and the world around them are real. We and the world exist independently from the whims, beliefs and imaginings of others or even our own imagination. Learning that this lovely world is real is a freeing experience. We can count on the world being there. We may not have experienced all there is to experience, but that does not prove the world does not exist. Another way of putting what students learn about themselves and the world is that they are both readers of text and makers of texts, which makes them responsible for who they are and what they are becoming. Reading and writing, in the broadest sense of both words, are what schooling is all about.

Brown and Campione (1994) wrote about discovery learning in a community of learners. Their research concluded that there is a profile for the ideal classroom, encompassing individual responsibility linked with community sharing. They found that "students in...learning communities are capable of deep, sustained, complex thinking, both in whole-class discussions and in their small groups." (p. 261) A community of learners makes it possible to contextualize and situate the learning activities so that shared discourse pays off with long-term gains.

Studies of the impact discussion-based approaches to developing understanding in English classrooms have found positive associations with engaged learning and successful interpreting of text. Applebee, et al. (Fall, 2003) report their findings from a study of 64 middle- and high-school classrooms in which discussion-based approaches were significantly related to high-performance literacy applications. These reports included both high-achieving classes and low-achieving classes benefiting from discussion-based approaches in reading and writing of texts. In general, their report supports our argument in favor of high academic demands linked to discussions and engaged-learning activities.

Becoming readers and writers of text, students learn that causation is real; namely that there are genuine relationships between actions and consequences. This is true of individuals and of society. The denial of causation is a basic denial of possibilities for changing the world for the better or worse and, therefore, a denial of accountability. Pinker (2002) writes about the depth of our rational faculties to analyze our experiences and maintain a sense of reality. He attacks the point of view that humans are "passive receptacles of stereotypes, words, and images" (p. 218) by those who would claim academic or cultural elitism over the masses. Pinker is especially annoyed by scholars who claim that there exists nothing outside of text and that we occupy a world of images rather than a real world. When we write that students are readers and makers of text, we do so in support of the reality of the world that our textual discourse would seek to understand. Pinker is right to declare that unless the world is recognized as real, it would "make it impossible even to identify lies and misrepresentations, let alone understand how they are promulgated (Ibid.)."

Engaged learning keeps us in touch with the reality of the world; objects, animals, other people are not our invention. They become text when we seek to understand the world outside of us. This constant interaction between the outside and the inside is the very stuff of learning. The student "checks things out." Do things fit? Do they make sense? Do they remain constant or are they changing? We are equipped with different kinds of knowing and reception. So, we have variety of senses which scholars make into "systems, modules, stances, faculties, mental organ, multiple intelligences, and reasoning engines (Pinker, 2002, p. 219)." To make the most of these faculties of mind, educators seek to develop dispositions in students to meet problems as opportunities for rational discourse. Art Costa (and his colleagues) calls these dispositions "Habits of Mind." (2000) When Costa's list is examined what one finds is a collection of strategies for active learning about the world.

They are the basic skills of thinking and ruminating about our experiences and what makes them so special for us is that they constitute exactly what we mean by academic fortitude. And it is precisely these habits of mind which are missing in marginalized students who get into college. They do not know how to use these skills to think about the world.

This discrimination is rooted so deeply in American society that we often do not recognize it. When African-Americans or Native-Americans are denied active and engaging learning, what they are being denied are the thinking and coping skills that make for the academic fortitude that all students need to succeed. Basic in what is missing in the marginalized students' educational experiences are the mental tools to deal with the academic and cultural world. Pinker makes this point about contemporary educational debates most emphatically: "Together with all the moral, empirical, and political factors that go into these debates, we should add the cognitive factors: the way our minds naturally frame issues." (2002, pp.221).

Pinker reminds us that we do not have to go to school to learn to walk, talk, and recognize objects or make friends and enemies. What we go to school for is to learn the skills of a written language, science and mathematics, all knowledge developed recently by the human species. Teaching academic subjects to students is not easy. Imagine the difficulties of teaching formal mathematics! Add to the problem of the innately difficult subject is the common teacher's fear of mathematics, even arithmetic. Teaching teachers to think about their teaching strategies, we could always turn off the class of elementary school teachers studying for their master's degree, by using mathematics example strategies in our instruction. The class would suddenly turn cold and literally stop thinking.

Pinker explains that education is not always fun: "...because much of the content of education is not cognitively natural, the process of mastering it may not always be easy and pleasant... (p. 223)."

Teachers find it difficult enough to teach reading, writing, and arithmetic; adding the demand for thinking skills seems too heavy a load to carry. One way teachers try to lighten their teaching load is by tracking students. If one sorts out students by tracking, what happens is that those who already know how to read get to practice at getting better at reading and writing. Others, who have not yet learned to read, are given worksheets and the most boring of activities to keep them from interrupting the teacher. We have observed the teacher in tracked classes taking the readers and turning over the non-readers to the teacher's aide or classroom volunteer. Discrimination grows within the school schedule, not so much by intentional bad treatment of minorities, but by the focus on the successful students which leaves the marginalized students behind. Those who are behind, get less and less attention and more and more behind. Missing are the academic skills which make for fortitude and survival.

Gerald Graff is a professor of English and education in Chicago and writes in his book, *Clueless in Academe (2003),* that school obscures rather than enhances the life of the mind. Essentially, he says that the focus on facts and lists does not permit students to develop the skills of discourse and argumentation. The temptation for teachers is to turn even non-factual questions into one right answer response. For example, if a teacher asks, "What is the symbolism represented by the Mississippi River in Mark Twain's *The Adventures of Tom Sawyer?*" The teacher's guide offers a right answer and that is what is fished for, instead of seeing the question as an opportunity for discussion and conversations about meanings. Repeated factualization of the curriculum throughout a public school career practically debilitates students when they face college and are expected to enter into the debates about interpreting the physical and literary world. Without the experience of academic discourse, students are incapable of academic conversations and they expect to find the right answer and go on to the next question. Because the marginalized students are more dependent on the culture of schools for their success, focusing on factual learning and high-stakes tests makes them even more incapacitated when faced with the college. Graff asserts that all American students could do better in school. He writes, "The college curriculum says to students, in effect, 'Come and get it, but you are on your own as to what to make of all of it' (2003, p.3)."

The teachers themselves are often trapped by their own teaching enterprises. Many education scholars have commented on the "loneliness of teaching." David Labaree (2003) describes the teacher trap this way: "Unless they work in an unusually collegial school culture, they can be confined to one classroom with one group of students without access to what is going on in other classrooms with other teachers and students (p. 20)." As a result, teachers can believe that there are no theories or generalizations as to what works or does not work in schools. Believing there are no theories about successful school teaching confines one to intense privatization in one's work. This is evident when one visits a teachers' lounge and listens to what teachers talk about: if they talk to each other at all, teachers tend to talk about their personal lives—and not about their professional work.

The result of teachers thinking about their teaching as a private business dependent on their own private experiences is what Labaree describes as "the primary bank of professional knowledge...being grounded in their own conception of moral purpose and their own style of personal engagement with students (Ibid.)." As a result, teachers tend to limit their understanding of teaching as experiential. Without a theoretical base for understanding their practice, teachers will see their own teaching as the only standard they know. Holding on to one's personal experience as the answer to all questions about what works in classrooms is like factual learning; it leaves the teacher with only one right answer as to how to do what they do. Likewise, teachers so oriented will tend to see each of their students as unique to their classrooms. Some students succeed, some students fail, such teachers will say. As a result, teachers' expectations for students are based on their own historical experiences with students they have taught. The cycle of discrimination and neglect will continue under such conditions.

What is to be done? If this is the case for even half of the teachers in America, how can we expect schools to improve? We believe that the gap between teaching and research that Labaree describes so well is like the gap between science and the humanities, in that over the years the two cultures have failed to create common ground. Few communities of discourse have matured to acknowledge the advantages each side of the arguments provides for the other. Stephen Jay Gould, in his last book before his death (2003), wrote about the communities of good communications between science and the humanities benefiting humanity in general. "Science needs the humanities to teach us the quirky and richly subjective side of our enterprise, to instruct us in optimal skills for communication, and to place proper boundaries upon our competencies..." (p. 143). Likewise, the humanities need access to scientific information to judge the reality of the world we all seek to improve. Only by overcoming the gap between science and the humanities, can we work together to improve the human community.

Teaching and scholarship do have common goals to improve the human condition. But in order for that to happen we have to learn how to communicate and collaborate across classrooms, schools, colleges and universities. In the following chapter we deal with the power of collaboration that opens up a world and breaks down the isolations that perpetuate discrimination and injustice in education.

Issues and Questions for Chapter Four

History of Schooling

- Schools are communities of text and communication.
- Early examples sited in the Mosque and in the Monastery.
- The basic issues of schools were making sense of experience, including the community and its traditions.

New Learning Theory Evolved over the Last 20 years

- All learning, we have come to understand, is active and interactive, not a passive process of "received" understandings.
- The way information is learned, determines how it is used.
- Mindful learning (Langer, E., 1997) continuously creates new categories of knowledge, open to new information, and is self-consciously aware of more than one perspective in interpreting experiences.
- Meier (1995) discusses why her school at Central Park West was such a success: it was small and the smallness made it possible for is everyone to know everyone else.
- Meier's students took charge of their own learning and presented in public portfolios of their work.
  Key ideas in defense of Learning Communities:
- The Importance of Peers in Child Development: (see: Harris, J., 1998) the role Offers new ways of thinking about how to organize learning, emphasizing the role of peer socialization in student learning; humans,

whether adults or youth feel better when closely associated with other humans.

- Learning Occurs in Contexts: (see: Bruner, J., 1996): Not only does learning occur in contexts, but what is learned stays connected to the original context; Bruner argues that not only what we think, but how we think is linked to the cultural context of the learning going on.

- Ideas as Tools: Pragmatism is basically an American philosophy, as exampled by Peirce, James and Dewey They all believed that ideas are not out there waiting to be discovered, but tools that people devise to cope with the world in which they find themselves.

- Fear of Failure is a Trained Response: While fear is a natural animal instinct, fear of failure is trained by ones circumstance. Mistakes are sources of learning. If we cannot learn from our mistakes, we are doomed to being victims.

- Teacher as Coach versus Teacher as Virtuoso: Contrast Asian teaching as giving a performance versus Western idea of teaching as coaching and encouraging the learner. A performance implies the students as audience and learning as copying the master. "Be like me!"

"Breaking up the Way into pieces,
Assigning ten thousand labels,
Breeds confusion. Enough of bits and lists!
Knowing when enough is enough
Keeps the class safe.
The way is to community
As the sea to a river;
A powerful invitation."
No. 32 The Tao of Teaching

CHAPTER FIVE
The Power of Collaboration

Americans have long believed in education as an investment in protecting democracy. Westbrook (1996, p.130) quotes Alonzo Potter, a 19th-century reformer, as defending the common school as the best defense against the common man. "The best police for our cities, the lowest insurance of our houses, the firmest security for our banks, the most effective means of preventing pauperism, vice and crime, and the only sure defense of our country, are our common schools..." A common school for everyone in our society calls from us a commitment to education that is unparalleled in human history.

Democracy requires of its citizens a shared understanding of the common good. That requirement does not mean citizens have to agree about the strategies for achieving the common good, but they must agree about the compelling idea of a common good for all in a democratic society. This understanding assumes that public discussion, debate, and discourse engage the citizenry about the national and local problems to be solved. Open discussions are critical to achieving a state of affairs that enriches, renews, and shares a common good for all. Robert Bellah and his colleagues write (1991) about the role schools play in supporting political discussion in a good society. "There is an obvious tension between schools as machines for the production of competitive, skilled workers and schools as learning communities of the creation of citizens (p. 264)." We join Bellah in seeing schools as learning communities and what goes on inside schools as a collaborative undertaking in engaged learning at all levels.

Individuals lose attention to the public good if they do not have the support of institutions. Again, Bellah (1991, p. 268) writes: "Without sustaining institutions that make interdependency morally significant, individual attention becomes fragmented in focus and delimited in scope." Museums, theatres, libraries, churches, symphony orchestras, and other public institutions provide the framework of support and exposure of the arts for a city's population. Individuals without art and articulation cannot function in a genuine democracy. Communities, therefore, support and provide for a broad range of engaging experiences. Stimulation of the mind and moral imagination makes for a growing and responsible citizenry. Schools are a part of this fabric of community that marks the character of a society. In many places, the schools are at the center of the community and provide the telling features of the social and political organization of the community.

A substantial range of agreement about what constitutes the common good can be understood as the culture of a community and unfortunately cultural assumptions can carry both good and bad consequences. A majority of a group or class of citizens can evolve a culture of oppression on various other minority groups. When assumptions are not tested but held as absolutes, it is difficult to change or reform the pattern of oppression. The tenacity with which a majority culture can hold onto oppressive behaviors against minorities is hard to break; it becomes "the way things are done, here." When that happens in such an organization as a school, nothing ever seems to change. That is why the patterns of marginalization of minority groups have become engrained in many school districts. Decades can go by and lots of rhetoric about justice and fair play can be uttered, but nothing changes.

For example, consider Franklin K. Lane High School in Brooklyn, New York. Reporters for the *New York Times* (Medina and Lewin 2003) tell the story of the school's discharging of over 900 students from the school as being too old (18) and too truant to warrant any continuing support for the teaching staff. Even though the law in New York State allows students to attend public schools until they are 21, the Franklin K. Lane High School says it has given up on these poor students by pushing them out to auxiliary services and equivalency programs in the New York City school district. The teachers and administrators say that nothing can be done to help these students academically and that they are taking up the time and resources of faculty that are needed for hard-working and needy students. "The pushouts are not the top students. They are the ones who skip classes, hang out in the halls, get into fights or do not show up at all for days on end (p. A21)." Clearly, the school just does not want to deal with them. Yet, for most of these discharged students this action is the end of the educational road. The school administration seeks to defend its actions as the result of current economic and academic necessities. But, wait a minute! This organizational behavior has been going on for the better part of a half century at Franklin K. Lane High School. The school's population is currently 3000, down from 4500 five years ago. But the school has been practicing discharges for many years. In 1969, the school expelled 670 students for truancy (Ibid.). A judge ordered these students reenrolled and required the city to provide tutoring for these students to catch up. So, over and over in cycles this school has used the same practice to keep enrollments down and ease the so-called pressure on teachers. Incidentally, the majority of these discharged students are blacks with few economic resources. The problems at this Brooklyn school are repeated in urban communities throughout the nation. But, to be denied schooling is to be denied access to participation in the economy, the social and political community and, for many, opens the way to a life of crime and/or welfare dependency. School policies can become tools of oppression, marginalizing students to an extreme, and eventually evolve into a part of a community's cultural values.

When there is no face-to-face interaction and no open discussion of policy within the community, then closed decisions (or conspiracies) get made that easily exclude the marginal students. Such is not a democracy when the values that support such oppression of a portion of the population are justified on absolute grounds with no way of testing the consequences of holding them. A major difference between positive and negative collaboration is that positive collaboration is usually open and public. Open collaboration makes it possible for everyone who wants to contribute to participate.

Schools need not divide and control students into classes and groups of competing individuals. Cooperation and group learning are powerful supports to students as they explore who they are and what they are becoming, as well as understanding the world of others. Some teachers complain that cooperative learning is too hard and does not work in preparing their students for high-stakes tests. However, Robert Slavin (1996) has spent a scholarly career demonstrating that cooperative learning is an effective instructional strategy. In particular, Slavin has reviewed in class ability-grouping at both the elementary and secondary levels (1996, pp 139 & 179) and has shown that "the effects of comprehensive ability-grouped class assignment *on student achievement are zero.*" (emphasis added) One of the major problems with ability-grouping is that if a class is divided into three ability-groups, the contact with the teacher is reduced by two-thirds. This means students spend a lot of unsupervised time on seat-work problems or projects— a situation that can be detrimental to student achievement (Brophy & Good, 1986).

Slavin and his colleagues did find support for across-school ability-grouping in reading, also called the Joplin Plan. This practice does permit teacher instruction time for each group, as the teachers across the school are assigned to groups. So, it is clearly warranted to conclude that reducing heterogeneity within classes to form homogeneous ability-groups does not improve student achievement, while at the same time, has detrimental psychological effects on students placed in the low-achievement group. On the other hand, the Joplin Plan builds on team work within collaborative heterogeneous groups. It shows evidence of producing genuine student achievements; principally by connecting learning to real world activities. Embedding the content of classroom activities in real world issues and community affairs is made possible by collaborative grouping.

Westbrook portrays Dewey as the defender of education for all in a democracy where all citizens are entitled to an education that will enable them to make the best of themselves as active and equal participants in the life of their community. He quotes Dewey (p. 137),

> *"Men will long dispute about material socialism, about socialism considered as a matter of distribution of the material resources of the community...but there is a socialism regarding which there can be no such dispute—socialism of the intelligence and the spirit. To extend the range and the fullness of sharing in the intellectual and spiritual resources of the community is the very meaning of the community"* (Westbrook, 1976. pp. 444-445)

So, for Dewey, democracy means creating community and sharing common issues and ideas. It then, follows that people are entitled to have access to the community and the processes that shape community. Schools are the major resource for achieving community equity. Currently, Americans are told by our national leaders, including some educational experts, that we must choose and support the elite few over the many in order to get quality. But, are the experts to be trusted? Americans, by and large, fear the elite intellectual, while at the same time they fear the concept of the common man. Current Dewey bashing in educational policy writings exposes the fear of an ignorant and irrational public as dangers to stable communities and institutions. Many so-called educational policy experts do not share Dewey's belief that the world has suffered more from leaders and authorities, than from the masses. Dewey believed that most men and women could become active participants in the decisions shaping their lives (Westbrook, 1991, p. 544).

Nonetheless, the current emphasis on accountability and

mandated state-wide curricula undermines the collaborative nature of democratic schooling. "At the heart of the ideological shift is an attempt to define academic success almost exclusively in terms of capital accumulation and the logic of the marketplace (McLaren, 1989, p. 5)." McLaren attacks those who would define school reform in terms of procedural management of school time and instruction, while, at the same time, they would define school failure as individual student failure. So, these experts would insist that "Academic failure ... lies in the genes, character traits, or home lives of the students themselves, hence unchangeable (p. 225)." Once again, we are face to face with the tendency to blame the victims for the failures of organizations, and the short fall of social justice. "In the prevailing view, social conflicts are reduced to individual, subjective concerns rather than as problems having to do with social and material inequality and collective greed and privilege (Ibid.)."

For many of the marginalized students, it is necessary to link cultural socialization with their identity development to improve educational achievement (Lee, et al., 2003). Carol Lee and her colleagues write about... "the need to integrate cultural socialization and identity processes into learning." She has evolved a program of "Cultural Modeling" to achieve such linkages in the curriculum and students' identity development. "Cultural Modeling is a framework for designing instruction that makes explicit connections between students' everyday knowledge and the demands of subject-matter learning (2003, p. 7)." Lee acknowledges the powerful idea that all knowledge challenges the learner's identity. Specifically, who we are and who we think we are is always at risk when we learn something new. That is why it is so hard and uncomfortable to learn new ideas; they challenge our old assumptions and what we thought we knew. New ideas and new helpful information will make us over into new people. So, the careful attention to identity formation by teachers is a critical concern in creating collaborative curricula. Developing academic fortitude helps students to accept their emergent identities. In contemporary school curricula, "African-American youth must constantly cope with subtle and overt manifestations of racism that may or many not vary by such factors as social class, skin color, gender, and body size… (Lee, 2003, p. 9)." This is why Lee urges teachers to focus on race as a social and political construction that influences the lives of African-Americans daily.

In developing learning communities in their schools and classrooms, teachers can create with students a new culture that cares about the developing identities of all the community's participants. In a learning community classroom, the discourse invites participation and helps students see themselves in action within a new culture. This new culture provides a caring environment for the evolving identities so students can risk trying out their new ideas, information, and understandings. Douglas Macbeth (2003) encourages the systematic study of naturally occurring classroom discourse. But we have known for a long time that the best teachers elicit from their students "risky conversations" about topics that may appear strange to their students. The verbal intercourse of classroom talk provides a platform for collaboration as students speak and listen to each other as well as to the teacher in the struggle to fit their minds around new ideas. So we see the process of classroom discourse as essential in promoting collaboration and in the search for new understandings, especially if students are to own their new ideas and find a manner for expressing them openly within the safety of a learning community.

One of the interesting realities of living on the margins

is that it can be a safe hiding space. Maxine Greene uses "margins" in this way to talk about art on the margins of social discourse. Indeed, many would consider art on the margins, as entertainment, perhaps, but not of practical use. Greene refers to Denis Donaghue when he speaks of arts on the margins, "a margin is the place for these feelings and intuitions which daily life doesn't have a place for and mostly seems to suppress...with the arts people can make a space for themselves and fill it with intimations of freedom and presence." Greene comments (1991, p. 1), "The idea of making spaces for ourselves, experiencing ourselves in our connectedness and taking initiatives to move through those spaces, seems to me to be of first importance." This is extremely true of learning communities. Learning communities provide the concrete and emotional space for exploring ourselves and our connectedness. Art is a tremendous arena for exploration by those who see themselves "on the margins."

Maxine Greene invites us to share a vision of schools as open and larger meeting places for all the population to come and participate. Listen to how she expresses this vision:

> *We ought to reach out to establish ateliers, studios, places where music can be composed and rehearsed, where poems and stories can be read. There might be new collaborations among questioners, as teachers and students both engage in perceptual journeys, grasp works, and words as events in contexts of meaning, undertake common searches for their place and significance in a history to which they belong and which they invent and interpret as they live. (p. 16)*

The idea of schools as learning communities and the

work of schools as collaborative learning centers reaches out to include those who have been treated as marginal students. It also addresses the concerns of those who worry about social control of adolescent energy or exuberance. Communities create the need for balance and reciprocity in order to exist. Individuals who see themselves as members of a community understand they have a role to play in preserving the community and supporting other members within community. Ivan Illich's interesting book *Tools for Conviviality* (1973) seeks to define the border between individual freedom to control one's personal energy and the ethical needs for social control. "I consider conviviality to be individual freedom realized in personal interdependence and, as such, an intrinsic ethical value (p. 11)." Illich is suspicious of the trend toward social progress that relies on technology to solve human problems. He believes humans have to use human community to explore their individuality. We cannot become well defined individuals without community and learning the benefits of what he calls "conviviality." Illich seeks to reverse the trend to megasocieties. "This reversal would permit the evolution of a lifestyle and of a political system which give priority to the protection, the maximum use, and the enjoyment of the one resource that is almost equally distributed among all people; personal energy under personal control (p. 12)."

Collaboration makes possible students' experimentation with their personal energy under personal control. To survive in a community, individuals learn to collaborate to preserve the possibilities of new journeys and discoveries. The teachers may help define some of the limiting parameters of the classroom community, but primarily as participants rather than controlling director. What teachers control are themselves as practicing participants in the learning community. What students learn to control is their own behavior, both overt and covert, if they are to experience maximum satisfaction from their participation in the community.

America's dream was the evolution of a community in which citizens could strive for justice, peace, fairness and compassion. We are still striving. We still must deal with those who believe all governments are a hindrance to individuals achieving self-control, or self-governance. But, this is a misunderstanding of Emerson's concept of self-reliance. He knew that community was the forum within which we as individuals could exercise self-control and reliance on self-command. Still, it takes community to develop and to test self-government. Schools have had this role and served it well for most of society. Those on the margins have not been served as well by schools; thus, we see the need for school reform. We believe school reform must and always be local reform, because all knowledge about human beings is local. We know what we experience and what we experience has time and place, the here and now. Knowledge about the here-and-now, therefore, is always local. The big mistake of the current national efforts of school improvement through achievement testing is ignoring the local context of learning.

Another problem in school curricula is the general neglect of the liberal arts in favor of practical courses and technology. If students are to enter college with a good measure of academic fortitude, they need the support provided by a liberal education. James Freedman (2003) connects the liberal arts with the strengthening of the democratic instinct in students. He writes of a liberal education that "…[i]t does have the redemptive potential to heighten the glories and exhilarations of life, as well as prepare us for its trials and anxieties. It has the capacity to enable us…to see the world clearly and steadily, to be conscious of the desirability of qualifying what we say with the word 'perhaps'.... (p. 70)."

Higher education needs to rethink the idea of a core curriculum, heavily invested in the liberal arts. The current emphasis on credentialing and certifying a technically sound future employee leads to a thin, crusted veneer of learning, rather than with depth of understanding for self and for the world at large. Isaiah Berlin attacks the Platonic history of intellectual institutions as valuing the product more than the process, the diploma more than the student learning. Berlin believes that institutions are all too willing to trade today's needs for tomorrow's promises. As a result, ideals and outcomes are valued higher than small progress to local knowledge. Institutional suppression of public criticism and debate is a way to justify the necessity of autocratic aggression; thus, it is no wonder that quantification leads to measurement and comparative analysis. So, it is also expected that institutions of higher education in America will focus on the achievements of individuals as evidence of valuing the institution. There are exceptions with a few colleges and universities that support collaborative group achievement, but most institutions praise their products, highly expert individuals who represent the new elite of the marketplace in America. Nicholas Lemann (2000) demonstrates convincingly that meritocracy is not part of the American dream of equality and justice for all. "The founders of American meritocracy were not supporters of an expanded, opportunity-oriented (rather than selection-oriented) educational system, and they were certainly not the originators of the idea of equal opportunity (p.351)." The meritocracy of the carefully selected graduates of America's major universities turn out to be a small governing elite who carry themselves and act very much like the old class elite system they replaced. Still, a quarter of the American population is left on the margins of the American dream.

Collaboration has the power to change this non-democratic meritocracy system. Collaboration works among teachers and students in schools. Collaboration between schools and colleges can work to redefine the school curricula and college entrance requirements. Collaboration works because it is inclusive rather than exclusive; it unites, rather than divides, and extends, rather than limits, individuals. Those, who collaborate in community groups, feel the strength they derive from each other within their group: without giving up their own power, they get to share the larger power of the group. Belonging to a group extends a collaborator's identity rather than limits it. Gangs know this and it explains why they are so successful in marginal neighborhoods where there is little security with one's personal identity.

Steven Levitt is an economics professor at the University of Chicago who studies interesting questions using amazing skills in statistical analysis. He is interested in many puzzling questions, e.g.: What is more dangerous to have in your home, a gun or a swimming pool? It turns out that the swimming pool kills more by ten times. Here is another question that intrigued Levitt: what really caused the crime rate to plunge during the past decade? His answer: Roe vs. Wade. Yes, abortion options for young urban women gave teenagers a choice so that unwanted children were not born. "Unwantedness" leads to high crime rates (see Stephen J. Dubner, August 3, 2003). The story is interesting on many levels, but clearly Professor Levitt's linking the crime rate and abortion is brilliant, and it highlights the importance of the feeling of belonging, of being wanted, and included. Without it, an individual and the society in which he/she lives is in trouble.

Collaboration in learning communities celebrates our

human belonging. One of the problems implementing collaboration is the resistance teachers have for sharing their students with others, but also sharing their authority over the curriculum and what students must learn. Teaching in America has been such a private vocation that teachers find it hard to give up their closed, tightly controlled classroom environment. Currently, teachers by and large do not have the skills to resolve conflicts, to share the learning, to organize without dominating, and to remain open-minded toward student achievements.

Holland and Mazzoli (2001) describe the massive efforts of one school district to improve student achievement on high-stakes testing and to revitalize the secondary school curriculum. They created a Freshman Academy in which special attention was given to students learning essential academic skills to be successful through the final three years of high school. They included algebra in the academy curriculum—at a very high cost—because students were not well prepared to take algebra. Still, they eliminated courses in "Everyday Math Skills" and "Pre-algebra." With great effort they were relatively successful, but at the cost of teacher resistance to expanding the design of the Freshman Academy to the subsequent years of high-school experiences. Their book makes for interesting reading because it lays out clearly how much work it is to change schools for the better. One of the leaders of the reform was brought into the urban school district from the outside. She knew that having a good plan was not enough, but that implementation was the essence of improvement. There had been a long history of talk about improvement in the district, but little had happened. The writers report the situation in this way: The new administrator... "[m]ight have encountered controversy in Gladston, but she also inherited a system that had stifled its underlying tensions for years, pushing problems below the surface but rarely solving them. She was the bearer of bad news, not the cause of it (p. 250)."

This, unfortunately, is a fair description of many school district efforts of reform. Talk among administrators at the top of the responsibility ladder has focused on reform for a long time. But rarely do they implement their plans or, if implemented, stay with them in follow-though efforts. Most schools that have tried to reform their curriculum found out that the price of reform is intensive changes among teachers and their relationships to each other and the administrators. Holland and Mazzoli summarize their study this way: "The haphazard implementation of reform explains why so few initiatives survive once the start-up funds dry up and why most haven't spread to other schools and school districts." (Ibid.).

The curriculum reforms of the post-Sputnik era in the late 1950s and 1960s should have taught us the lesson that new and interesting curriculum isn't worth much without implementation. John Rudolph reviewed the movement to upgrade science education in the schools after the shock of Russia's Sputnik circling overhead. Massive nationwide efforts were invested in rewriting school curricula in science, mathematics, English and foreign languages. The Physical Science Study Committee (PSSC) created a terrific new science curriculum. Such major universities as Massachusetts Institute of Technology (MIT) invested in rewriting curricula and the products of these projects were clearly superior to the old curricula. The National Defense Education Act (NDEA), beginning in 1958, provided over a billion dollars for college support. Foreign language institutes followed with the Educational Professional Development Act (EPDA) with the effort to raise the standard and number of foreign language graduates from American universities. Throughout all this massive effort over two decades much good was achieved with some individual teachers and in some schools. But, by and large, the curriculum reform failed to achieve its goals. Many new science curricula were left on the school laboratory shelves, and teachers returned to their old and familiar ways of teaching chemistry and physics. Math Skills for Life courses continued to be popular as teachers avoided algebra and focused on skills for balancing bank checkbooks or doing household budgets.

The influence of the local culture of a school district is always powerful. "They way things are done" is always a powerful commentary on proposals for change. There are those in academia who would maintain a cynical attitude toward the possibilities of genuine school reform of any kind. Clifford Geertz describes such critics as those "who stoutly insist that nothing ever really changes in human affairs, because nothing ever changes the human heart, about how to deny that it (*renewal*) is actually emerging (2000, pp. 221-222)." He describes these "postmodernists" as critics without hope for positive change. "There are, so it is said, no master narratives, about 'identity,' about 'tradition,' about 'culture,' or about anything else." (p. 222) If we are to believe these critics of change, there are no visions that, if held, do not lead to prejudice and, ultimately, conflict. And yet we are reminded that knowledge is local and full of details and concreteness.

> *"Those of us who are committed to sorting through concrete matters so as to develop circumstantial comparisons—specific inquiries into specific differences—may seem naïve, quixotical, dissimulating, or behind the times. But if guidelines for navigating in a splintered, disassembled world are to be found, they will have to come from such patient, modest, close-in work." (Geertz, Ibid.)*

The work of school reform is one arena of human endeavor

that needs exactly the close-in work Geertz describes. We are not prepared to abandon hope for the American dream in education. What we need are efforts in local politics that go deeply into the community and its cultures to negotiate a way out of elitism and cynicism into a realm of collaboration for reform.

Again, as we have observed before, we believe the world is real, even if we cannot always see a real world nor understand what we see. So, we side with Hilary Putnam, the Harvard philosopher, and not with Richard Rorty who would have us believe that to say something "is true" is just a "compliment" we pay to something we agree with. Putnam says, "Cultural relativism of the Rortian variety is antagonistic to the strain of 'scientific realism,' which holds that only science tells us what is 'really' there; in fact, it is antagonistic to the very notion of being 'really' there." (1989, p. 69). He goes on to say that a person need not "give up on the idea that words and sentences are *related* to things and happenings in the world (Ibid.)." When one admits that our words are reliable then we can say that what we have described is "true." So it is, that we can make the effort to say what we mean and mean what we say as we experience and describe the world.

The issue of reality, so briefly addressed here, is linked to the debate about the character of learning itself. Phillips and Soltis (1991) present the argument that would define learning as a change in behavior (pp. 83-84). They would argue that talking about learning as something that goes on in the head is not very useful to a teacher. But, it is possible to confuse the "evidence of learning" with the learning itself as a change in a person's understanding. The quality of learning is hard to measure by quantitative means. Individual learning is often best expressed in a community of fellow learners, but that does not make the learning going on a public behavior. The occasion of the articulation is, indeed, a public event, even though the learning is a private interior affair.

In a world that is full of uncertainties and difficulties, there is a certain lack of courage on the part of those who would give up on the world as making any sense whatsoever. Clifford Geertz offers his wisdom, again, on this issue. He advises us that if we are to deal with the world seriously and have something useful to say about it, as in school reform, then the differences among us must be see, emphasized, dealt with directly. It is a mistake to see our diversity as a metaphor for the complexity of universal values covering up an underlying oneness. Geertz emphasized that the common identity of humanity is located in our diversity, one group from another. Difference must be valued as the very construction of our identities. *(see:2000, pp. 226-227).*

This work of negotiating who we are in our differences that Geertz describes, really begins in schools with collaboration. The collaborative effort to build discourse about who we are and what is going on is a good place to begin, to affect school reform. We must acknowledge our differences, our diversities, our growing cultures and personal identities. To create communities of learning, the collaboration of all the participants is needed. So, no one can be excluded and treated on the margins. What collaboration does in a classroom and, ultimately in a school district, is that we illuminate one another. We speak the words of exploration of the realities we experience. We come to recognize who we are and, even more important, who we are becoming.

We do not have to label each other, either culturally or

pedagogically. Labels are only useful for tracking those we wish to keep at a distance from us; a distance that is from the center of things to the margins. Pushing some students to the outer margins is the product of labeling and the theories that invent their meanings. But, if differences are recognized explicitly and candidly, as Geertz advises, then we can deal with who we are and what we are trying to do collectively in our classrooms and schools. Collaborative classrooms open up the exploration of valid information. In discussions we can listen to the voices of our students and teachers making free and informed choices, because collaboration frees up the self-protection mechanisms we usually exercise in combative and competitive environments. If we are not invested in self-protection, then we are free to learn and grow in the collaborative environment. In a caring environment, both students and teachers are free to take risks and try on new ideas without the fear of ridicule or rejection. In fact, the examination of ideas is the very essence of open discourse. The testing of ideas happens publicly and openly in the learning community. The differences among the individuals are recognized and are valued by the whole community as providing the rich resources of the group.

A large part of collaboration is the cooperation that takes place across institutions and across classrooms. For example, there is the Achievement Via Individual Determination project (AVID) in San Diego, as reported by Barry McLaughlin and Beverley McLeod (1996). In the public high schools low-income Latino and African-American students are getting the attention and guidance that is usually reserved for those students going to prep schools. AVID is an "untracking" program that takes students of high potential but who are currently suffering neglect in low-track classes, and puts them into college prep courses of study. In addition to their regular classes, "AVID students attend a special class where they are taught how to take notes and study for tests, and where they are personally encouraged, guided, and coached into going to college." (1996, p. 13). Given this special attention by teachers in the project, the students experience the emotional support they need to consider college in their future. As a result, 88 percent of AVID program graduates goes on to college, compared with 71 percent of all city high-school graduates. When they find an environment where they receive the support and encouragement as well as the skills for survival they need, students often respond positively. Such special programs take planning, commitment, and resources in order to succeed. In other words, it takes collaboration among the teachers and administrators to bring off such positive results.

The collaboration among institutions that is necessary for genuine educational reform is just more difficult to achieve. We proposed a "Summer Success Academy" in northern Michigan for minority students heading into community colleges and state universities in the following fall. The plan created groups of minorities, including Native-Americans, Hispanics, and African-Americans at different sites around the state. Ferris State University would act as the leader among the institutions while the programs developed a model that could be disseminated around the entire state in subsequent summers. Besides specializing in the core ethnic historical and contemporary material, the academies would focus on what we called developing academic fortitude. We planned sessions on note-taking, research writing, how to avoid plagiarism, the protocols of college advising and meetings with instructors. Our goal was to help prepare students for college entrance with both positive working skills and positive self-images. The plan was not supported at the very highest levels of state and university leadership. They thought that what we proposed was the job of the public schools and that remedial help to students was letting the secondary schools "off the hook."

Similar actions occurred in Massachusetts at about the same time. The reform plans crafted at the State Board of Education level were voted down, with the deciding vote against the proposal by a major university president. It turned out that university leadership was anti-reform, pro-competition, pro-skills testing and rote learning for developing mathematics skills. Progressive reforms were seen by college officials as "touchy-feely" stuff. This is not surprising as most universities are anti-democratic in practice. The lofty ideals about the university being a bastion of freedom and defender of democracy is expressed in theory, but in practice the leadership structure of most universities in America is hierarchical and autocratic. Just try to get something done on a Big Ten campus that the president of the university opposes! So, in practice, universities are against doing what is necessary to create equity and fairness of opportunity among its potential students. Once students are admitted, many universities offer some form of remedial help. But few universities take any leadership in developing and recruiting students from the margins of the state's population. Many of the colleges within universities are territorial and anti-cooperative. Much of the higher educational reform is confined within colleges and not shared with other colleges on campus. The biggest example of this phenomenon is in the information technology game. At the heart of the university, collaboration is not much practiced and the students suffer the consequences. Also suffering the consequences of inter-college competition for funds and programs are the temporary instructors who are doing more and more of the university instruction on college campuses. Over half of the faculties in major universities are now in non-tenure stream temporary positions with no future commitments by the university and very small, if any, benefits.

We may be tempted by cynicism, but what we need is a recommitment to the public good, a basic democratic idea. Again, we quote Cornel West (1999) who wrote: "a democratic sensibility cuts against the grain of history... To be a part of the democratic tradition is to be a prisoner of hope. And you cannot be a prisoner of hope without engaging in a form of struggle that keeps the best of the past alive." (p. 308). We become "prisoners of hope" when we admit that though success in our struggle for educational reform and a just access and programs for all American students is not in our grasp yet, we must persist in the struggle nonetheless. Cornel West must have been tempted by despair many times in his brilliant academic career as he is widely attacked across the spectrum of academic and political values. Yet he persists in the pursuit of his vision of the democratic tradition in higher education.

We believe that collaboration in learning and program development is a fundamental democratic process, and it embraces the cultural diversity of our society. Basically, we agree with Clifford Geertz in his position which he describes as "Anti-Anti-Cultural Relativism." (2000). Many voices in America over the last decade have attacked the so-called cultural relativism of our diverse society. William Bennett is against cultural relativism; Chester Finn and Allan Bloom both have taken anti-relativist positions and written in favor of a position that only can be called "cultural absolutism," a view that maintains there are eternal truths and moral absolutes that apply to all times, people and places. Such total nonsense does not force one who disagrees into a cultural relativist position that would say nothing matters, that there are no values one can defend. We agree with Howard Gardner (1989) when he says that goodness and beauty are concepts we value, but that holding such values does not lead us to the same behavior, or the same reality or experience in every situation (p. 269). One can believe there is a divine being without signing up to a particular religion! Religions, like political parties, are social phenomena. Spirituality is a matter of interior quality of life. If we lie to ourselves often enough about who we are and what we believe, we kill spiritual adventures. The temptation to religion often comes in place of killed spiritual explorations. Sincerity has nothing to do with it; after all the Spanish Inquisitors were sincere believers! Culture is relative because we are all different and our ethnic histories are different, but that does not make us relativists in the sense that nothing matters. Culture very much matters (See Harrison and Huntington, 2000).

We believe culture to be a living, growing, creative part of being human, not some by-product of our socialization. Our lives are complex, no matter what ethnic or racial background we inherit. We live and move among many cultures, and saying one is better than another is like saying one religion is better than another. China's economic expansion is a major example of a multi-cultural country seemingly shifting toward self-expression and democratic values. Ronald Inglehart (in Harrison and Huntington, 2000) describes the current Chinese communist leadership as an elite clearly committed to one party rule; but they maintain their control over China with military power. As the cultural lives of various Chinese ethnic and geographical groups experience economic growth, the preference for democratic institutions also rises to the surface and, over time, democracy will become an issue linked to cultural expressions (p. 95).

Cultural diversity and collaborative values are essential

to democracy. Though rich countries are more likely to be democratic, there are many rich countries that are decidedly not democratic. Essential to democracy are cultural patterns of participation in public discussions and decision- making. Democratic institutions survive and flourish because of the commitment of ordinary citizens to democratic values, not because some elite leadership maneuvers to reform organizations or institutions. The cultural differences among us in America are a source of our strength and lead us to share public values in justice and fair play, social caring, and tolerance and well-being. The differences among us are more common than the similarities among us. When we engage in educational change/ reform we must embrace the differences that characterize our cultures, how we live our lives, and what we may be able to see. Looking for the lowest common denominator among us to find what makes us similar will not succeed as a starting point for change. Start, rather, with our most radical differences and our most outrageous claims about ourselves and the values we hold if you want to open up avenues of change. Talking and thinking together about our differences are the keys to collaboration in building learning communities.

In the chapters that follow, we will explore how students get access to colleges and universities. We believe that there are specific tools for access that students can master if they are taught successfully how to use them. Furthermore, we will have to face the issues that arise out of what Mosley calls "the dead hand of history;" that is, how individuals in communities can change their fate and create their own paths to successful lives. Finally, we will return to the central issue of curriculum, its construction, its interpretation, and the dangers of the easy choices in what we teach.

Issues and Questions for Chapter Five

Democracy means Face to Face Communities

- What are some of the reasons that democracy requires a shared understanding of the common good?

- Do schools have a mandate to create good citizens as well as produce good workers?

- Why do individuals depend on the support of public institutions?

- Museums, theatres, libraries, together with schools provide the framework of support and exposure of the arts; because without art individuals cannot function in a democracy. Schools are part of the creative fabric of community.

Cooperative Learning

- Are schools designed to divide and control students into classes and types of competing individuals?

- On the other hand, cooperation and group learning are powerful supports to students exploring who they are and what they are becoming, as well as understanding the world of others (Slavin, R.,1996).

- Dewey (1898) argued that the very meaning of community is to be found in extending the range and the fullness of sharing of community intellectual and spiritual resources.

- Must one choose the few over the many in order to get quality? Are the experts to be trusted? Americans, by and large, fear the elite intellectual, while at the same time they fear the concept of the common man.

Collaboration Enlarges Community

- With the arts, people can make new spaces for themselves. Art is not merely entertainment. Making spaces for ourselves is the very nature of citizen participation in community.
- Maxine Green invites us to share a vision of school as open and larger meeting places. "We ought to reach out to establish ateliers, studios, places where music can be composed and rehearsed, where poems and stories can be read..."
- Illich (1973) seeks to define the border between individual freedom to control one's use of personal energy and the ethical needs for social control. "I consider conviviality to be individual freedom realized in personal interdependence and, as such, an intrinsic ethical value." (p.11)

Democracy as the pursuit of happiness?

- What did the founding fathers mean by the phrase: "pursuit of happiness?"
- What was meant by the phrase that the best government is the one which governs least?
- Schools, according to Emerson, are to develop in each new generation the capacity for self-government and self-reliance
- What value does a liberal arts education contribute in a technical/material world?

Can the Academy serve marginal students?

- Why do institutions of higher education so focus on the achievement of individuals, while valuing the institution more highly than people the institution is designed to serve?

- The Platonic history of intellectual institutions values the product is more important than the process.
- For many academic institutions ideals and outcomes are valued higher than small progress to local knowledge.
- Institutional suppression of public criticism and debate is a way to justify the necessity of autocratic aggression.
- Quantification leads to measurement and comparative analysis.

"Can you love your students
Without demanding their affection?
Understand, without interfering?
Provide structure, without binding?
Give birth, Without claiming heirs?
Teaching influences, Without dominating.
A good teacher leads
Without creating followers."
No. 10, *The Tao of Teaching*

CHAPTER SIX
Tools for Access

We have been documenting and pleading the case for special treatment for students who are currently outside the mainstream of American education; these students we have called "marginalized students" are not marginal human beings, but they have been made marginal in their skills and understanding necessary for academic success. Here, we believe the keywords are "have been made," as they are often under-prepared and uninformed about the protocols necessary to succeed at the post-secondary level. For example, *Washington Post* columnist William Raspberry reports that some minority and marginalized students are falling behind their classmates by "as much as four years by the time of high-school graduation" (*Washington Post,* October 13, 2003). We have argued the case for improving the treatment and attention to these students and, thereby, improving the school experience of all students. Much of what we have to say in this chapter, while directed at solving the problems faced by marginalized students, also makes sense as guidelines for educating all students.

Most important, though, is to attend to the needs of poor, minority, and first-generation students attending college or applying for college entrance. We believe that a special service unit is needed to support collaboration among schools and universities in identifying student early in their need for special help. The tools these students need to gain access to academic success at the college level takes time to acquire and the earlier that students are identified as being in need of help, the more likely collaboration between schools and colleges will succeed. The tools for access are the basic ingredients in developing academic fortitude in these students and include both cognitive and affective understandings about successful learning. This is not merely a special plea for helping marginal students; rather we are asserting that all citizens in a democracy have a right of access to public wealth. Dwayne Huebner (1997) asks the difficult question: "How do we make the public wealth of this world—the traditions, knowledge, information—accessible to all children?" (p. 135) We believe that special efforts must be made now to reach out to the marginalized of our society and bring them into the school academy. In doing so, we will discover that we have found answers for improving schools and colleges for all students, whatever their background, tradition, or class.

The American Council on Education (ACE) presented a statement to the U.S. Senate on October 17, 2003, entitled: "Promoting Access to Postsecondary Education: Issues for the Reauthorization of the Higher Education Act." While the statement has all the hallmarks of a reasoned and careful document, the really interesting feature of this statement is that it focuses almost totally on finances. The ACE seems to argue that money is the main issue, maybe the only issue, in improving access to higher education. We know that money is important, but wait a minute! Money is not the main issue in helping marginalized students gain access to postsecondary education. Money is secondary to the substance of an education that would indeed give students access to a university education. We remain dedicated to the substantive reform of higher education if we are to improve the lot of marginalized outcasts in our communities. In fact, one could argue that a focus on money assumes that it is the lack of money that excludes marginalized students from postsecondary education. Some students may be fully qualified and need only a scholarship to succeed but, by and large, it is not the main issue. What is missing in the education of these students is reading mastery, facility in mathematics, problem-solving and logic, study skills and a sense of the adventure of learning. If a person has these qualities, money is not an issue; some way will be found for them to enter university.

Ferris State University (FSU) has faced many problems with under-prepared students and created a "Strategies Program" to help students gain the tools of access to successful academic careers. Many of its students, who are also first in their families to attend a post-secondary institution, come from isolated rural areas and declining urban communities in Michigan where their school experiences have tended to be factual memorization and skill acquisition, rather than concept development, problem-solving, and understanding of self and the world. These students typically have limited mathematics experience; they do not understand their own heritage; they have little understanding of modern literature or the classics; they have usually not experienced much joy in learning and discovery. In other words, they possess no academic fortitude in solving the problems of higher education curricula. Raspberry (2003) suggests that these students might understand the importance of an academic credential, but often avoid the challenging courses and perform at levels that are "good enough" without being committed "to excellence." We agree with Raspberry's main thesis; but disagree that these students are not seeking challenges. The marginalized students are often under-prepared because they often do not know about the challenges nor are they prompted/motivated to perform at high levels. Further, these students are products of substandard K-12 educational experiences that do not engage them in meaningful learning and so they pass through the educational system without having their critical needs met. So, FSU created an orientation class FSU 101 for everyone and Structured Learning Assistance (SLA) sections for specific classes. The SLA sections offer specific support for the students. This support includes special review periods during which trained tutors review the professors' lecture, outlines, materials, etc. to prepare the students to succeed

A FSU professor reported that she encourages her students to use their voices in every class, because they have had little opportunity to share their voices in the past. She believes that the more they hear their own voices and know that others hear what they say and accept and respect their ideas, the more they will participate in class discussions. With participation and engagement comes a sense of the empowerment of learning, she believes.

One of the biggest shocks marginalized students receive when they enter any university system is to discover the open-minded, higher-education environment is dramatically different from their community cultures and previous schooling. Rarely do university professors take attendance. Rather than lecturing on attendance and assignment policies and encouraging their students to study, professors state their expectations in syllabi, which go unread by the students who are unaware of their importance. Professors assume that students are adhering to their syllabi, which they consider to be learning contracts. Most assignments are for long-term accomplishments, rather than requiring the daily submission of brief and limiting assignments. The measurement of long-term accomplishments is particularly problematical in mathematics and foreign language classes for the under-prepared students who are used to being monitored on limited bits of skill acquisition. As a result, students find they can miss classes and no one will say a word; students can fail to turn in assignments on time and no one is going to call them to remind them. Students are expected to be self-disciplined, organized and persistent if they are to succeed. The students who do not put themselves on a personal study schedule, comply with the expectations described in the syllabus, and work at a steady pace throughout the semester, are not likely to succeed. Many practice late-semester cramming, but few succeed by depending on that strategy. Often, the new college student is also facing the problems of being away from home for the first time; they are developing social sensitivities in an environment that is diverse and strange to many of them. The distractions of college dormitory life are powerful. Everything is happening at once. Getting enough sleep is often a major problem for students. Failure is easy to come by!

Many of the marginalized students have a background in which they were tested on tiny bits of factual information and, as a result, never grasp the entire conceptual framework of the disciplines they seek to learn. In other words, they learned to focus on the parts but not the whole of a subject. Furthermore, these students often complain that their professor did not test them on the information that they studied. They usually read their assignments after the professor's lecture, focusing on the information told to them by the professor; so, their knowledge is not constructed by their own inquiry.

The Strategies Program at FSU seeks to help students learn how to decode the mysteries of college protocol. To plumb the depths of higher education requires students to learn how to organize their lives, using a calendar to help them make choices and creating a schedule of priorities in order for academic tasks to be done. Working-class families often believe that success in college is the result of inherited qualities; and while we are not dealing here with the nature versus nurture issue, we believe that by the time a student is entering college it is too late to worry about inherited qualities. We can, however, work on acquired habits of mind and self-discipline skills. Successful time management, for example, is not developed by gene inheritance, but is an acquired skill and it makes a big difference in the quality of work a student may produce.

Some of the work of the Strategies Program is simple. When students follow their associate deans' and counselors' recommendations that they take advantage of this service, they participate in an interview and a series of assessments, including a vision screening. Interestingly, many students referred to the Strategies Program have undiagnosed, correctable vision problems that, perhaps, plagued them throughout their past academic history, because many K-12 districts eliminated vision screenings after kindergarten as part of sweeping budget cuts.

Academic fortitude is constructed out of the tools of access over time. The first and most important set of tools have to do with the basic skills of literacy: reading, writing, oral communication, mathematics, and scientific principles of exploration and discovery. Without these basic skills, much of the other tools are useless. For example, without algebra, calculus is impossible. Without calculus, most science courses in higher education are impossible. When students do not possess basic mathematics skills, we know we have a potential failure written all over the student's record. People may say that they do not need algebra to succeed in life, but that is not true in today's high-tech culture. In a sense, without fundamental courses, such as algebra, students have incomplete prerequisites for future courses. Similarly, without the ability to analyze, solve complex problems, and engage in discourse, students do not have the prerequisites for academic success. Graff (2002), specifically, argues for improving the students' ability to engage in academic discourse and that, without it, students cannot connect with college-level learning.

Literacy skill development is a lifelong exercise. Reading, learning a second language, writing and researching papers, preparing and giving oral presentations, all have a powerful influence on a student's academic success. Plagiarism is a particularly significant example. Academic cheating has become so common that students often will argue with professors that "everybody does it." An article by an English department professor (Edmundson, 9/9/2003) discussed how to curtail cheating on essay assignments. He recommends that professors should ask better questions. That is, he argues, analytical and critical essays are easy to buy on Internet sources, such as, DirectEssays.com. But, "If professors asked students not only for analysis, but also personal, reasoned responses, they would,

I trust, get fewer purloined papers." He is right, of course, asking students to be engaged personally with a subject or topic or a particular event does make the assignment more relevant and, as a result, produces higher-quality responses. Literacy problems are solved by practicing personal literate responses in all the forms of language. They are certainly not solved by state-mandated curricula in phonics reading instruction based on "scientific" practice in teaching reading. Frank Smith (2003) demonstrates the flaws and fallacies in the claims made for phonics as a necessary step in teaching reading. He points out that sounding out the alphabet has nothing at all to do with learning to read. Basically, he says, reading is making sense of the world and writing (p. 10).

In addition to the basic skills that make for academic fortitude, there are other tools that can be taught as self-conscious strategies creating access to success. As Raspberry (2003) suggests, attitude, which is part of the self-conscious strategies, is critical in one's approach to study. Most of these tools have to do with the thorough development of personal self-consciousness. We may be born with a consciousness of ourselves and the world, but self-conscious monitoring that corrects perceptions and makes possible for us to learn from our experiences is an acquired skill. This capacity creates a continuing self-monitoring tool that assesses what one is experiencing by examining the link between action and consequences. Thoughtful reflection on one's actions and their consequences is a mark of an educated person. The "O, spontaneous me!" approach to living may be thrilling, but it is cheap because it is easy. A person who takes the "Popeye" position of "I am what I am," basically does not take responsibility for the connection between cause and effect of one's actions. Developing personal self-consciousness involves observing the effects of what we say and do on others and teaches us how to modify what we say and do in order to achieve responsible consequences.

Teaching self-monitoring exercises to students may seem trivial when compared with the study of the so-called nuts and bolts of facts and skills. However, colleges and community college are troubled by the number of students who enter college without a sense of who they are and what they can accomplish academically. The problem is so widespread that many schools are doing what we are recommending in this work, namely creating collaborative school and college projects to help minority students. For example, in Manatee County in Florida, the Manatee Community College (MCC) has a unit named Edison College which runs special programs reaching out to area high-school students to help them prepare for the rigors of higher education. Edison College has an Upward Bound program for poor students with limited home support in academic achievement. These are mostly first-generation potential college students who need to learn how to succeed in high school. MCC also runs a program called the Summer Bridge Program to help students from low-income families make a successful transition from high school to college. Edison College has found that their students need to continue mentoring in reading and in self-monitoring life skills over time.

To support these efforts, MCC has formed a task force designed to have annual meetings among teachers in schools and the faculty at the college. They focus on mathematics and language arts in this task force. The task force hopes that communication between and among educators at the high school and community college levels will improve. Edison College at MCC administered tests to students graduating from high school to determine their preparedness for college-level courses. The college found that less than half of the students tested were ready to do college work. The students may meet state and county high school diploma standards, but a majority of them cannot do college level course work.

Northwestern Michigan College (NMC), a community college in northern Michigan, has a similar program for non-traditional students who have high-school diplomas, but cannot do college-level work. Although the focus of the NMC Bridge Program is developing academic competencies, the Bridge participants learn about academic fortitude and become empowered students. When they are empowered, the students make appropriate choices and monitor their learning progress. Another key to the success of the NMC Bridge Program is goal development. Many of the participants entered the program without having life goals; rather they lived for the moment or the next paycheck, until they got involved with the Bridge Program.

This problem is not an isolated problem, but more definitely a national issue. The basic issue is this: if a student does not acquire his or her own tools for constructing meaning in the academic world, they cannot compete. What we are saying is that the acquisition of the tools of access in education is not the main focus of public education. The main activity that goes on in schools is listening to the teachers and following directions. Some teachers know that they have to teach directly about the tools of access: for example, reading is a lifelong tool that must be taught directly to most children. Some children acquire the tool of reading on their own while listening to their parents read to them. Others live in a reading environment and learn from their siblings. But, for most, reading is a mystery until teachers address the process directly. All tools help us connect with the world. Eric Booth (2001) writes about the tools artists use to make it possible for them to connect with the world (p. 78). Making connections with the world creates access to meaning. Reading is a tool that, when acquired, provides a lifetime of pleasure and capacity to understand the world by participating in the world. The participation is the self-reinforcing engagement with the world that tools make possible for humans.

What Booth is talking about with his discussion of artistic tools is the way acquired job skills can humanize people when they bring to us personal satisfaction and meaning. We learn to enjoy our work, become engaged in our work, because it expands our vision of who we are and what are the possibilities. Of course, most adults have to earn a living, but Booth speaks of artists as those who "yearn a living (p.253)." His point of view about tools has relevance for our discussion of the tools of access to academic success, because educators have come to know that the best motivation for students' learning is intrinsic. By intrinsic motivation we mean the joy of learning, the pleasure of engagement, and the satisfaction gained from understanding how things work, all of which push students to work harder in their studies. What a change in perspective it makes when students want to perform and be engaged, rather than having to be bribed by extrinsic rewards, no matter how pretty the gold stars are! And it changes how teachers think about students when they seek to invite students to the celebration of learning, rather than to the strict control of time and space.

Yet, the most feared criticism a principal can made of a teacher is that she does not have control over her students. One may know one's subject, work hard, and attend all the important meetings, but none of that counts, if her students are "out of control." Teachers fear that their students will become uncontrollable if given an inch of freedom. Polly Nichols (1992) describes this as the curriculum of control; without control it is argued, children have no chance at learning. So, much of what we have said about the open classroom and collaborative learning in the previous chapters is bound to be challenged by teachers; just as our ideas are viewed by many teachers as idealistic, unpractical, and worst of all "liberal." Our point is that the entire emphasis on control of student behavior in schools is misguided and at the root of the problem. Except in prisons, true control is ultimately self-control. Nonetheless, control remains an issue for many educators. Parker Palmer (1998) describes the whole enterprise of education as riddled with fear, as students fear to fail or be laughed at, so teachers fear losing control over the class. Palmer said that even "After thirty years of teaching, my own fear remains close at hand... It is there whenever it feels as if I have lost control; a mind-boggling question is asked, an irrational conflict emerges, or students get lost in my lecture because I myself am lost (p. 36)."

The issue is how we may deal with our fears, both as students and teachers. Acknowledging that we teach with fear and trembling is one of the first confessions to make with our students. Then we can get on with teaching in such a way as to invite all students to learn by exploring the real world around them, including themselves and their fears, their fellow citizens of their school communities, parents, teachers, administrators... all of them. What is to be learned is substantial and not merely a focus on "modifying their behavior" to conform to the standards of adult obsessions for orderliness and quiet classrooms. Control then ceases to be an issue, even though we may never fully lose our existential fears.

A curriculum of control teaches students to respond to control, instead of engaging and interacting with the subject discipline they are studying. Regardless of the discipline or grade level, students need opportunities to participate in substantive conversation about their learning, make connections to the real world, explore the discipline in order to acquire deeper knowledge, and demonstrate higher order thinking about the concepts of the discipline (Newman, Secada, and Wehlage, 1995). When teachers engage students in such substantial conversations, students develop their own methods for making new conceptual connections, find new applications, identify different points of view, analyze problems, and synthesize information. Additionally, we contend that tools are needed to access academic success and these tools are precisely the tools students will develop when focusing on substantive issues and exploring the world around them. If students are not engaged in subject matter learning, they are denied access to knowledge and, ultimately, they will fail to develop the academic fortitude essential for success in higher education. Many students in American come to hate school as boring, petty, and trivial. Control of behavior becomes an issue when classrooms are cold and students are denied the joys of learning. Yet students can take a lot of boredom and triviality and still learn and enjoy their school. Young people are resilient and can learn under all kinds of trying conditions.

In contrast, Harold Bloom (2000) writes about the joy of reading and the pleasures of learning to read. He says that reading is the most "healing of pleasures." It is a personal and private resource that one carries throughout a lifetime. So, students who are denied the opportunity to learn to read and to read with pleasure are robbed of a substantial and pragmatic skill. Further, Bloom says "reading well is best pursued as an implicit discipline (p. 19)." He means that everyone develops his or her own personal methodology for reading in various contexts of life. But, of course, there are times early in life when we must approach reading as an explicit discipline. Time to read is also ways to read that come with practice. The school and the home can provide the opportunity to practice; and if the home cannot, then the school is the student's only hope, if one is to learn to read with skill and pleasure.

Still, Bloom is right to remind us that reading is an asset to strengthen the self (p. 22). In other words, reading is a tool of access, not only to higher education, but also to a larger and more interesting life. As with most tools, reading improves with practice and we develop our individual styles of reading depending on the context in which one reads. Ultimately, reading is a major tool by which one can judge for oneself the rightness or efficacy of an idea or value. When we learn to judge for ourselves, we embrace with confidence our capacity to gain understanding and explanation of ourselves, others and the world around us. Finally, the reader gets to know the writer well. The reader has access to the great human beings from the past to the present who have written of what they know and experienced. So, as readers, we get to know greatness and share the adventures across the pages of history. Reading is the core of liberation and that is why it has always been suspected by those who fear freedom and democratic principles. For centuries tyrants sought to control the free access to books and those who would read them. Censorship is still an ugly word; all readers are against it. That is why the Attorney General is so concerned in keeping tabs on libraries and who uses them and what the readers read. The American Library Association may be the last bastion of freedom fighters in America as they have taken the position that librarians will not comply with the federal Patriot Act provisions for computer lists of library users.

When we turn to the study of mathematics in our discussion of the tools of access to academic fortitude, we encounter a miasma of varied opinions. The love and hatred of mathematics and all the emotions in-between seems to touch everyone who has attended a school or academy. On the one hand, there is the view of Siméon Poisson, a French mathematics professor at the Sorbonne, who is said to believe that "Life is good for only two things, discovering mathematics and teaching mathematics." We are sure that many Frenchmen would disagree with that idea. At the other end of the continuum, there are those who hate everything about trying to learn algebra in high school. Some students learn mathematics as if they were discovering poetry. Others claim that nothing about their mathematical exercises ever made any sense to them, except the problems seemed to have been designed to drive them crazy. So it is a difficult subject even among educators, and particularly among mathematics teachers. The National Council of Teachers of Mathematics has written goals and objectives for K to 12 curricula, giving examples of the types and domains of mathematical skills that should be taught. However, one can find teachers of mathematics who do not think that mathematics should be required beyond the basic skills of elementary mathematics. Nel Noddings (1997), once a mathematics teacher herself, now takes the position that not everyone should be required to take the same mathematics courses in high school simply as prerequisites for college admission. Her argument is that, "at least in high school, we should provide different mathematics courses for students with different interests." (p. 330) But, at the very least, students must know about the mathematical world we live in. It is difficult to prescribe a curriculum for mathematics beyond the very basic arithmetic skills. Noddings makes it very clear that she does not advocate throwing out mathematics because it is not necessary for everyone at the same levels of usage (p. 332). At another level of advocacy for mathematics as a necessary tool of access, witness what Moses and Cobb (1999) say about mathematics education in the black community: "I believe that the absence of math literacy in urban and rural communities throughout this country is an issue as urgent as the lack of registered black voters in Mississippi was in 1961 (p. 5)."

One of the many problems with designing mathematics curricula for everyone is that some students seems to "get math" quickly and with ease, while the rest of the world struggles. Gardner (1983) has defined skills in mathematics as one of the major types of intelligence out of the seven or nine "Frames of Mind" of which humans are capable. He calls it logical-mathematical intelligence. For some people the capacity of object permanence comes early and forms the basis of logical and mathematical manipulation of the world. When we can think about something out of our presence, then we think about it abstractly. This abstract thinking is the beginning of mathematical skill, many would argue. The problem is that many minority children have difficulty with school mathematics. They do not take to drills and skills of school mathematics and many children come to fear and hate math. It is further a problem when it becomes clear that teachers—especially elementary school teachers—also treat mathematics with "fear and trembling." As a result, many a school teacher communicates her suspicion of mathematics in teaching basic arithmetic to her students. In fact, a colleague observed a primary teacher tell her young students that if they were to hurry through their arithmetic worksheet they could go outside to recess early and have fun.

To acquire the mathematical tools of access to academic success may very well mean that special training for the mentors and teachers of the development programs must also take on a thorough study of mathematics. They need to learn the fun in problem-solving and be an advocate for the uses of mathematics in the real world. We are committed to maintaining high standards in this area as well and not pursuing "second best" mathematics for dummies for students on the margins. Watered down courses of mathematics perpetuate the "second-class" academic citizenship that already permeates the discussion of school and curriculum reform for marginal schools.

One of the problems in designing mathematics curricula is the disagreement among mathematicians about the role of intuition versus axioms in learning arithmetic. Stanislas Dehaene (1997) reviews the efforts over the last century by mathematicians who would define mathematics in terms of axioms and syntactic rules. He calls this attempt as a formalist approach to mathematics. Russell and Whitehead were among the thinkers who championed the formalist approach. But Dehaene quotes John Locke who wrote: "Many a one knows that 1 and 2 are equal to 3 without having thought on any axiom by which it may be proved." (p. 241) He also calls on Poincaré who, in his work, *Science and Method,* ridiculed mathematicians' attempt to define integers through set theory. Dehaene concludes that the human brain does not rely on axioms. (Ibid.) Interestingly, in our own time educational researchers have demonstrated that elementary students are capable of discussing mathematics at an abstract as well as a concrete level. Our colleague, Deborah Ball taught a third-grade mathematics class at the Spartan Village Elementary School in East Lansing. She conducted the class as a community of mathematicians. Deborah Ball turned much of the mathematics agenda over to her students. She said, "There's a back-and-forth between reading about the work of mathematicians and watching and listening to eight-year-olds and trying to figure out what makes sense (Quoted by *Changing Minds,* p. 5)." The treatment of math as conversation marked the distinguished work Ball conducted during those 15 years of mathematics teaching and her work with Professional Development Schools at the College of Education of Michigan State University (MSU).

Noddings also demonstrated that high-school students can enjoy and master difficult and powerful mathematical problems. But she reminds us that if teachers are to teach to this level of mathematical discourse, they "will need a different kind of preparation from the one they receive now. They will need mathematical preparation especially designed for teachers." (1997, pp. 333-334). One effort to train currant mathematics teachers is reported by Jay Mathews (2003) describing the work of Kathy Kubic, the math coordinator for Anne Arundel County, Maryland. She and her colleagues have rewritten the K-12 mathematics curriculum for the entire county, in order to integrate the math teaching with the Maryland State Standards for mathematics. With new books and new guidelines, it was essential to conduct staff development for the math teachers. Kubic and team provided 16 hours of training with the new materials. However, 16 hours may not be enough for some teachers. One of the teachers says that these materials are the best thing she has seen yet for teaching mathematics for all kids.

Also, there are pockets of advanced mathematics preparation for teachers forming around the country (e.g. College of Education at MSU in collaboration with the College of Natural Science). Genuine collaboration between mathematics departments and teacher educators has been a rare phenomenon but it can work and does work when it is recognized that all academic departments in a university are responsible for the quality of teacher education on the campus. Chris Ohana (2003) describes the collaborative project developed at MSU called "Mathematics is Everywhere (MIE)." A major goal of the project was to create a university-school partnership that would contribute significantly to the improvement of mathematics teaching in schools and the preparation of mathematics teachers. While collaboration works at MSU and the MIE project, it will take a long time for such integration of curriculum and collaboration of university departments to become the standard practice across America.

We have been describing the process of acquiring the tools of access to academic success. But it is clear that we are not discussing a formula for producing success. Individuals and their communities produce success. What we are committed to is substantive change in the school curriculum for all students. Howard Gardner (1999) put it this way: "I want everyone to focus on the content of an education—the meat and potatoes—on how that content should be represented, put to use, and passed on to others (p. 16)." There is content to the tools we propose as essential for an educated person. The content includes what some might call merely procedures, but which we are convinced are substantial in their academic content. For example, in the Strategies Program we connect with the high schools and emphasize listening to the multiple voices of our culture. Literacy includes listening with respect to the cacophony differences that make up the cultural background of each of us. This is a tool of access, learning how to respect and use the vast differences among us. It includes paying genuine attention to our own and others' identities; who we are and who we are becoming. We examine the ways by which we can understand what is happening around us. We do so by making the familiar strange and the strange familiar. We ask questions about who are our fellow students, our colleagues, our friends? What do they expect of me? What do I expect from them? We take the time to write out the answers we get from the questioning process. Even factual writing about these questions and answers has a creative element through engagement with others and the world we live in.

Another way we work on putting the tools of access to the use so students become familiar with functioning in an academic environment is by examining, specifically, the protocols of college. We bring out and examine the college bulletin and the class schedule book. "What is going on here?" we ask at the start of the decoding process. In a sense, we put our students into the detective framework of solving the mysteries of college/academic life. They examine the university policies that guide and define the roles of university staff and students. They look at a wide variety of course syllabi asking what makes a syllabus a good one. Can they tell what will be on the tests, what the instructor expects from students who take his/her course? The students also make up a schedule for attending classes, studying, working, playing and still reserve enough time for the essentials of living, such as getting enough sleep. In other words, we are deeply into the substance of moral and social values when we examine who we are and what we are becoming.

One of the insights that we learned from Gregory Bateson (1980) is that chaos and stability are always in struggle with each other. Basically, chaos is the natural condition in this universe and the human mind struggles to create understanding that brings some sort of stability to our world. Certainly, this is an accurate description of the experience of students entering college or university after high school. What they encounter is a vast complexity of the seeming chaos of higher education. However, students with experience in organizing their experiences out of chaos and into some form of stability will succeed in making sense of out their first experiences in college. The high-school students, who were marginalized by their experience of public schooling, have much greater difficulties sorting through the diversity of a college campus and making sense out of it. Now this is not entirely a bad thing. The struggle itself can be the source of satisfaction and self-esteem for the marginalized when they have some of the hints as to how to decode the higher education environment. Academic fortitude develops when students learn to deal with chaos and how they can construct their own understanding of the world.

Every teacher knows that every class is different, as is every student and every year. The fact of diversity cannot be denied, yet every teacher's first impulse is to seek control over diversity and make it manageable. So, when teachers show that they are trying to cover up the chaos of diversity and teach the same stuff the same way, as though all students were the same, they communicate to students, especially the marginalized, that sameness is desirable, that control is a primary issue, and that students should be of one mind agreeing with the teacher. If a control vision of the world is what teachers present to their students, it becomes a source of great confusion about the chaotic world in which we live. Teachers may say they value diversity, but so often we forge toward sameness. We, fellow teachers, fear the impending chaos hanging over us, so we construct magical defenses to lock out chaos and bring predictability to our professional lives. But we always fail.

We fail because chaos is not some potential <u>out there</u> waiting to mess up our lives, but rather chaos is the very core of human experience. Chaos does not break into our lives from the outside, it rises up from within. Chaos is part of the process of living. Lorenz (1993) says of chaos that it is the appearance of random processes; that is, those variations which *are not random but look random* (p. 4). When we do not see it, we are kidding ourselves. We pretend that order and pattern are the norms and chaos is the exception. Actually, chaos is the norm. James Gleick (1988) has reported how scientists have learned that chaos theory offers profound guidelines for making sense of the world. What scientists are learning about chaos theory is what teachers must learn about their teaching. They must learn that not dealing with the concept of chaos publicly with their students is teaching students to believe in some sort of magic. Because the students know that we live in a chaotic world and when they see teachers pretending it does not exist, they feel left out of the secret to unlock the mystery. Actually, we do not know what to do most of the time; so we are tempted to reach for predictability; perhaps if we believe hard enough in some magic formula, somehow predictability will be granted to us.

Yet we can understand chaos differently, especially chaos in the classroom. We can understand chaos as the source of richness and variety characteristic of interesting and challenging curricula; curricula complicated enough to attract student curiosity and motivation for learning. When students learn that they can live with chaos and make small sense out of it a piece at a time, they become comfortable to be around multiple stimuli and the seeming chaos of our institutions and our universe, including colleges and universities.

One of the realities teachers must come to terms with is the variations within the communities in which they teach.

Over the last few years, teachers have grown more and more resistive to communities and families turning over the rearing responsibilities abandoned by parents to the schools. There are many seasoned teachers who see keenly the difference between the kinds of students they taught twenty years ago and the students that come to school today. Their parents want the schools—and that means the teachers—to do the total rearing job, but they resist any criticism of their children, and insist on a no "hands-on" guidance of behavior, accepting no failing grades of their children's work. It is discouraging, at best, for teachers. But we should remember that there was a time, not too long ago, when teachers were the lowest-paid, least-respected, and most-criticized professionals in the community. Some active community collaboration between educators and the parents of students must be undertaken, if connectedness and common goals are to characterize our schools.

Direct education about the social, economic and political structures of communities is sorely needed in the school curriculum. Students need to know the state of affairs of their communities which support the schools. Parents must share the burden of teaching social and educational values to their children. The reason for this is that the very knowledge the school would teach about the world depends upon an understanding of the corporate nature of human understanding about the world we live in. Knowledge is not a collection of data that needs to be stored in students' "computer-like" minds. Rather, it is intimately connected to the values and systems humans create. The questions students need to learn to ask about what they are assigned to learn are questions that make information problematic. Example questions would ask: "Where did we get these data?" "Who are the experts about this subject?" "What meanings can I construct out of these problems and this context?" "What heuristics (problem-solving strategies) have worked in the past in this context?" "Do they work for me?" Such questions take students on a journey far from passive rote learning to explorations and creativity. The questions are essential tools of access to academic success and lead students to become their own person within an academic environment.

Tools of access ultimately lead students to struggle with the critical issues of schools and society; questions of praxis (to use Friere's favorite word) and emancipation. Critical issues arise with the student's use of his or her own power self-consciously. Critical questions asked in the use of these tools are: "Who is in charge?" "What is the party line in this community?" "What can I do to change the power relationships for the better?" "What is just and fair in this context?" And "How do I test my own values against the consequences of my actions?" Successful application of this level of tools of academic access is a transformative experience. William Doll (1993) writes of the power of an integrated curriculum. He says in a new curriculum: "The focus would now be on a community dedicated to helping each individual, through critique and dialogue, to develop intellectual and social powers (p. 174)." Instead of the old three Rs (reading, ritin, and rithmetic), Doll advocates a new set of "Four Rs" in the curriculum: "Richness, Recursion, Relations, and Rigor (p. 176)."

A "Rich" curriculum would contain lots of the stuff of living, including the chaos, indeterminacy and community diversity of human life. "Recursion" refers to the iterations and repetitions of school experiences matching the living contexts of our communities. Recursion leads to dialogue and the double-looping Argyris (1982) described in producing effective learning. "Relations" provokes our awareness of the matrix of our knowledge, as well as our social contexts. What we know depends deeply on the network of information and its sources that surround us. Finally, "Rigor" is the feature of interpretation, because interpreting puts us individually on the line for responsibility for what we know and are coming to know. Rigor provides us with the tool by which we deal with the indeterminacy of life and our shifting relationships. Students who acquire these tools of access to academic performance will not be controlled by capriciousness of government policies. Nor will teachers be convinced by the national coercive pursuit of absolutism in the guise of benevolent schooling.

The tools of access to academic fortitude incorporate the emotional side of life with human rationality. Antonio Damasio (1994), a leading medical researcher, writes about the seeming contradictory "passion for reasoning." He claims our emotions and reasonings are intimately connected and his research seems to support the idea.

> He writes: *"...educational systems might benefit from emphasizing unequivocal connections between current feelings and predicted future outcomes, and that children's overexposure to violence, in real life, newscasts, or through audiovisual fiction, downgrades the value of emotions and feelings in the acquisition and deployment of adaptive social behavior* (p. 247)." Damassio.

The tools of access to academic fortitude, also, provide the security to construct a moral framework in one's life which can, indeed, protect one from the volume of vicarious violence that seems to dominate our society. We can make up our own minds. And we can construct a moral framework to interpret for ourselves what is good and just amidst the confusion and chaos that surround us.

We agree with Berliner and Biddle (1995) who argue that our schools are not failures and, in fact, that schools are improving and have been since the 1970s, expect for the marginalized and outsiders in our society. There are business interests in selling the idea that schools have failed because education is a trillion dollar industry and corporations want control of the spending of that kind of money. There is a sense in which the "No Child Left Behind" policies favor the private industrialization of the curriculum publishing, evaluation, and promoting of centralized educational standards. We believe that if schools and universities attend to the needs of the marginalized students of our country to acquire the tools of access we describe here, we will build the academic fortitude required for all students to succeed to the level of their individual goals, without centralized social engineering of America.

Issues and Questions for Chapter Six

Creating collaboration between schools and universities

- Creating successful students is a group effort and cannot be accomplished by focusing on one student at a time. A special service unit is needed to attend to the needs of poor, minority, first generation students attending college. This requires institutions to collaborate and identify groups of students early in need of support.

- The example of Ferris State University's success academy demonstrates that students from isolated rural areas and declining urban areas in Michigan were taught by focusing on skill acquisition rather than concept development and understanding.

- The short falls in preparation show that students typically have limited mathematics experience; do not understand their own heritage; limited knowledge of modern literature or the classics; experience little joy in learning, and show no academic fortitude to problem solve their academic predicaments.

Making up the difference

- Marginal students need the access skills to engage in higher education in an open minded environment. (Bruner, 1990)

- Bruner argues that self-awareness includes knowing what you know, and it makes a difference in how one teaches.

- If every knowing is only personal story-telling, there is no way to account for learners acquiring knowledge and shared understandings.

- Thinking about our thinking helps us choose the appropriate heuristic for a specific problem, discipline or situation.

Academic Fortitude

- Learning how to learn involves learning to decode the mysteries of college protocol.
- Most marginal students have never learned the skills of organizing their calendar, making choices including a schedule of priorities for tasks to be done.
- Working class families mistake success in college as a quality that "some people have and some don't." They do not see the processes of successful time management as a learned skill. Seems like a lucky break or an innate ability.

Literacy: Reading, Speaking, Writing

- Literacy is also developing one's voice, point of view, trusting ones own judgment, while remaining open to new ideas and experiences.
- Specific skills in reading, writing and speaking are high priority skills for marginal students to approach mastering in order to succeed in college. It is not finding the "truth" out there to report on, put developing truthful understandings.
- Confidence in all three skill areas makes the difference between success and failure.

Mathematics as an access tool:

- Problem Solving at the algebra level is a minimal coping tool for access to contemporary science.
- See the work of Henderson, R. and Edward Landesman who train teachers to take a thematic approach to mathematics instruction, e.g. focusing on common themes: architecture (bridges), astronomy (space), and statistics (baseball).
- Goals are the application of mathematics to concrete problems in the student's life.

Computers and Multimedia Skills

- Learning to use of library resources and technology to gain access to information and construct email support groups is crucial.
- New Technology brings new tools to the marketplace of ideas, so technology is both tool and content to be learned and used.
- Direct instruction and practice is necessary for groups of students to learn computers skills and communicate with significant others via email.
- The use of resources on the Internet for doing research for organizing papers and projects is a prerequisite.
- There is a need to develop open communication systems for the marginal student.

Struggle with the Class Schedule

- Developing a class schedule while decoding the college bulletin and class schedule book is a new task for most marginal students. They need to learn how to develop a personalized academic schedule of courses and times of classes.
- Students need practice in laying out personal academic

syllabi using problem solving operations, including: analogies, logical and deductive rules for one.

- They also need to know how to synthesize information, testing utility and focus on choices and consequences.
- All students are confronted with the need to develop schema for mapping out road to success.

"A community runs on justice;
Fair play becomes routine.
Contrast school administrators,
Whose tactic is surprise.
A community is achieved
By letting go of control."
No. 57, *The Tao of Teaching*

CHAPTER SEVEN
Communities of Hope

I f we are to follow Walter Mosley's (2000) exhortation to "shake off the dead hand of history," we must embrace hope that individually and collectively we can make a difference in our communities. Without positive attitudes and values toward academic success, it is not likely to happen, even as we recognize that hope is not sufficient in itself to create justice and a new world of opportunities for the marginalized citizens of our country. But we argue that the educators' job is to develop the gifted in each student and that means believing each student can learn. Such belief takes hope! We find it very difficult to understand how the cynical teacher can function in a learning community. If educators do not believe in and act for the positive improvement of the learning environment, who will? If the powerful are not compassionate and supportive of those without hope, who will be? It is our conviction that great things have happened to improve the quality of life in the educational community in America, but that we are far from reaching the whole population of American youth. There remains some 40 percent of the school population that drops out or does not go on to higher education and becomes, as a result, functionally unemployable in our society. It is almost as if the economy is bent on creating a Third World workforce inside America, where the pay to marginal Americans will be commensurate with what corporations are now paying to Asians. What can make a difference in such a gloomy picture? The answer is education for all.

A teacher education department administrator told us that hope was synonymous with education because people look toward education as a way to improve their lives. She then asked the rhetorical question: "Where is hope today?" The political winds of change are disallowing and closing schools where open enrollment and academic support programs give the marginalized students an opportunity to succeed and a chance for the good life. Simultaneously, state legislators are cutting support to higher education thus forcing colleges and universities to have massive tuition increases, and the federal legislators are cutting financial aid and loan options for those students. Consequently, the most economically needy students, who would add value to their communities and states by acquiring an education, are being squeezed out of the system. The result makes hope for the future nearly unreachable.

The argument of this chapter goes something like this: yes, race, gender and ethnic differences still matter; however, creating communities of hope is the critical response to injustice in access to academic success at all levels. Therefore, we argue that the task ahead is to gather colleagues of academics who share hope in the possibilities of reform and greater fairness; to do this we need to have substantive goals for all of our students, which means that for some of our students—the marginalized—more effort must be extended, because they start out behind the majority student body. Most of the marginalized are from blue-collar families and they experience college as first-generation students with all the baggage that carries. We aim at reaching for some sense of "belongingness" for all of our students. Our colleges and universities must strive to become the social and intellectual home for these students. This means educators have to dream and hope for not just improvement, but for achieving the best kind of education for all their students. The challenge to the faculty is to not accept the perceived role of second-class faculty when helping marginalized students advance. We reach for lofty goals, we celebrate each step along the way, because we know that each success breeds further advances toward a just and fair society.

Corporate America has to come to terms with the reality of the situation, as does academic America. We can no longer afford to tolerate the corporate pillagers of our resources; these barbarians who think they are above the hard-working masses and deserve to be paid millions of dollars a year and will still rob the corporate treasury. The larger community of American businessmen must find it in their hearts to believe in hard work and just pay for all, including themselves. Some may say that such remarks are out of bounds in a book about educational reform, but we believe there is an intersecting corporate wholeness to America and that what happens on one stage influences what happens elsewhere. American school children may be a lot of things, but they are not stupid. They see the business pillagers ripping off their own companies and they say, "You see, everybody does it." We are paying the price even now, when youth would rather not work at all, if they cannot make big money. The example of the pillagers in our society does not go unnoticed, in fact, they teach cynical lessons about the waste in study and hard work. Still, one must believe it is possible to overcome such outlandish models of behavior, just as teachers must compete with the entertainment media for the attention of their students. Even as the food and beverage industry in America pushes its sugar- and fat-laden products on school children (see: *Fast Food Nation*. E. Schlosser. 2001), we must believe that educators can make a difference in the face of such powerful cultural influences on youth. Hope, however, is the necessary ingredient; not only my hope and yours individually, but whole communities of hope are required, if we are to surpass surviving and go on to thriving in creating a new and just world.

Nevertheless, the corporate executive mind often undercuts the very purposes of the organizations they serve to the detriment of their communities. One of the current examples, to make our point, is our old friend the Kauffman Foundation in Kansas City. Ewing Kauffman was a businessman who amassed a significant fortune, owned the K.C. Royals baseball team, and was grateful to his community for his successful life. He was especially grateful for the education he received in the Kansas City public schools. So, Kauffman created a foundation whose goal was primarily to aid and improve the quality of life and educational experiences of Kansas City citizens. Since his death, the Kauffman Foundation value has grown to something in the neighborhood of $1.6 billion. (See Strom, S. 2003, *The New York Times*) Now, the interesting detail: the new foundation chairman, who after eighteen months still commutes to his job in Kansas City from Baltimore, has ambitions to make the Kauffman Foundation a bigger player on the national scene. He has fired local employees and hired high-priced consultants (e.g. at $500,000.) to give him advice to achieve a national prominence. A foundation that started out to support education, that created a scholarship program called Kauffman Scholars, that contributed heavily to the Kansas City school budget and other local projects, is now headed on a course to become a big-name foundation (even though its assets rank it as 27th out of national foundations). Things are a mess in Kansas City. The point, of course, is that the American businessman's loyalty to bigness and not necessarily the best is corrupting the local commitments and sponsorship of education in Kansas City. The students in the classrooms of the Greater Kansas City Community are watching all of this and they know they are being betrayed by the powerful, once again.

So, it is easy to be tempted by cynicism when it comes to believing in the American dream of a just and fair educational opportunity for all citizens. However, in this last chapter of our work, we seek to set in perspective how small, positive efforts and small "pockets of hope" (de los Reyes and Gozemba, 2002) can indeed change the world. In the process we will review some to the critical issues we have raised in the previous chapters and how we propose to deal with them in concrete, even small enclaves of classrooms and academies. We know that learning must be understood and dealt with in terms of both the individual and the community (Anderson, 2000). They cannot be separated meaningfully, so the goal of positive change in our schools is an expression of our communities of hope. There is no meaningful academic development without individual development. Just as the architectural plan is not the building, nor the map the same as the country, so the name of a program like "No Child Left Behind" is not the reality of the education experienced by many individual students in our school systems.

Even though much of the curriculum of the classroom is mandated either by district, county or state agencies, the fact remains that it is the teacher who must decide what to teach. In choosing what to teach, the teacher is expecting to choose something "good to teach." Teachers must, in turn, explain to students the grounds for believing something is "good to teach" and therefore, "good to know." We believe that the issue of choice is connected closely to the process of engaging students in the learning tasks. The teacher has the primary responsibility for creating quality in her classroom; there can be no equivocation on that point. Of course, the students count, as do parents and community values; everything counts. When teachers choose substantive material to teach, they may not know a final explanation for their choice, but they must know why they chose what they did in order to explain to the students why they believe something is good to know. Even if science doesn't have the final word, it doesn't excuse the teacher from teaching the little we do know. We can follow Dewey's (1910) advice and teach students to be reflective rather than reactive. Dewey argued that we should welcome the surprises, puzzles, and perplexities of life with our curiosity. In this point of view, Dewey clarified the essential notion of the scientific method. He wrote: "The function of reflective thought is, therefore, to transform a situation in which there is experienced obscurity, doubt, conflict, disturbance of some sort, into a situation that is clear, coherent, settled, harmonious (pp. 100-101)." Basically, Dewey taught us to "endure suspense" as a motivation for searching for answers.

We may not have final answers as to what is the best or even the most desirable teaching materials for our students, but that fact should not leave us defenseless. We do have experience, we do have knowledge about what has worked for us, and we can defend our choices by some kind of tests for educational value. The process of making choices for what we would teach can have some tests for high-quality curricula. We can list some of the ways teachers have been making choices. Such a list has the pragmatic function of spelling out what we believe to be desirable consequences, if not the "Truth" in some absolute and abstract sense. Here is our list of tests for educational value.

1. *The test of time.* Is the material, book, play, poem, text, etc. enduring? Is it something that people have been coming back to over and over again and finding value in it?

2. *The test of simplicity.* Is it simple? That is, is the material straight-foreword and requiring only simple explanations? Simple explanations are often more useful or effective in instruction than complicated ones. Simple does not mean plain or unsophisticated. For example, Shakespeare's *Hamlet* is full of fairly simple ideas which have stood the test of time.

3. *The test of depth.* Is the material profound, moving, not trivial? Depth is not about complications, but about interest and impact. For example, *Death of a Salesman* is a simple story, but as a play it has profound impact on audiences. The exploration of literature by our imagination can provoke continued quest for deep knowledge and understanding. Allington (2000), for example, argues that students need to discuss the ways the text is related to them, to other texts, and to the world beyond the printed text.

4. *The test of uniqueness.* Is the material unusual, not vulgar or common? Something is special if it is

so unique there is nothing else like it. It begs for inclusion in the curriculum of high value.

5. *The test of utility.* Does the material have useful effects? Does it do something informative? Does it engage the reader and learner actively rather than passively? Is it fun? Do readers get enthusiastic about the subject or specifics represented and enjoy the experience?

6. *The test of explanation.* Does the material explain something? Does it offer a look at a theory or concept or principle that is not found as clearly elsewhere? For example, an Interlochen Center for the Arts mathematics teacher told us that he does not use high-school textbooks in his classes, because there are no explanations in them. He uses college math textbooks which contain broad explanations of how and why things work the way they do in math. He believes that the traditional mathematics instruction in high school leaves students dependent upon the teacher for explanations. If students develop a dependency habit, even in mathematics, it is difficult to break later on.

Good materials and the challenge of perplexity help the teacher invite the students to develop the traits of carefulness, thoroughness, and thoughtfulness. Instead of jumping to easy conclusions, the curriculum should teach students to "turn things over" in their minds.

Some critics of school teachers and educators would have us believe that all society wants from schools is good babysitting until the child is old enough to fend for him/herself. We will always have such critics, but the professional educator expect trivial critics and knows to ignore them. Teachers also know that society needs the capacity to create responsible citizens for each generation and democratic schools are fit organizations to fill that role. Our forefathers had the vision that a democratic form of government involves its citizenry with active striving for justice, peace, fairness, and compassion. What was really meant by the idea that the best government is the one that governs least is a government in which there is plenty of room for individuals and groups of citizens to exercise self-government. The role of schools is to develop in each new generation the capacity for self-government and self-reliance. And the role of universities is to prepare accomplished professionals who can lead the citizenry in all arenas of public and corporate life.

Communities of hope strive to fulfill this vision or dream of American success. When we reiterate the goals of American democracy, we do so in hope, rather than believing we have completed the journey or finished the task of building a just and fair society based on a just and fair educational system serving all of the citizens of the state. Emerson distinguished between the party of memory and the party of hope. He meant by this distinction that the cynics of society celebrate the past as evidence that the American dream of justice for all is impossible to achieve. But it is the worst kind of cynicism to counsel that since we have not been successful in the past, there is nothing to be done in the present. Hope exercises our humane center and excites the prospects of equity and justice for all. To win, we must learn, does not mean somebody else has to lose. This is particularly true in the academic domain; students who gain knowledge and competence do not deprive others from the same access to understanding. It is clear to us that our schools and universities must be linked meaningfully to assure equal access to education at every level in America. Tom Watkins, Michigan's former Superintendent of Public Instruction, recently said that "neighborhood public schools are the nursery of our democracy. Neighborhood public schools give us hope and opportunity (2003)."

Communities of hope also need agents, mentors, or facilitators, who can make connections with the "marginalized students" and help these students plow through the foreign trails of academe to find the path to success. We heard Harold Hodgkinson, the famous demographer, speak to a group of educators at the Association of Independent Michigan Schools (AIMS) Conference in 1984, when he urged each member of his audience to volunteer to help one marginalized adolescent achieve success in school. Nineteen years later, at the Michigan Governor's Educational Summit, we reminded him of his plea. He said that the adolescents of today need caring adult mentors more than they did in the past. Just like our examples of the young man who went to Ferris State University because a teacher assisted with his application for admissions and financial aid and that of Joseph Aguerrebere whom we met in the first chapter. Dr. Aguerrebere, a first-generation college student from East Los Angeles, made his decisions about college according to the color of the football uniforms, proximity to his home, and financial aid. He had no knowledge of the quality of the programs or his place in the milieu. He also relates his experiences as a first-generation, post-secondary student from an urban high school where he had no one to guide or prepare him for his encounters in college like so many other students from similar backgrounds and environments. For him, academic success would have been elusive without his developing relationships with professors and others who could point the way and interpret the language to him. Simple directions like "fill the blue book" were incomprehensible to him.

Antoinette is now a junior in college; however, her first year was a very difficult adjustment. She arrived at her college from an under-funded, large urban high school where she had permanent substitutes for key college preparatory classes and few experiences that prepared her for the rigor of college. When she was failing and ready to give up, a member of the university administration became her mentor. The mentor helped her with time management, directed her to key tutorials that helped her to succeed, and functioned as a listening-ear, devil's advocate, and friend. Without the relationship, Antoinette would not be attending the university, thinking about a study-abroad program and applying for teacher certification.

The early establishment of student-adult relationships is one of the main reasons that the first-year college orientations programs are successful. Often, faculty who participate in the first-year, orientation programs are fairly young and closer to the students' age. These are people with whom students can develop connections and maintain relationships throughout their college experience. The orientation faculty member often becomes the student's advisor and, as we know, good advising is another important feature in retaining students through graduation.

Both administration and faculty need to know about the marginalized students' predicaments and their struggle against all odds to persevere. For example, a senior, Leonard, like many caught in the squeeze between funding cuts, tuition hikes, and financial aid reductions, has three part-time jobs to pay for his tuition, living expenses, and books. Yet, he attends every class and submits all of his assignments. Unfortunately, his professors merely report that lately he has seemed fatigued and often dozes in class, so the quality of his work is slipping. They do not understand his struggle. If they did, they would learn that he really has a positive attitude and realizes that if he keeps working through the year he will graduate and reach his goal of achieving a baccalaureate degree. He has hope, but can the hope sustain him through his financial struggle?

Zoe, a minority student from an isolated rural community, never stopped. She had difficulty comprehending, writing, and computing, but she sought help. Finances for Zoe, like Leonard, became insurmountable; in fact, she had such difficulty that she had to leave school to work. Other personal issues interfered along the way to a degree: her beloved grandmother, who was her caregiver and guardian died; her young husband was unemployed; and her children required her time. Yet, she continued working toward her goal of a college education, taking classes when she could afford them and working for the university to pay for classes. When her children entered junior high school, she graduated and found a professional position. She is the first person in her family to graduate from college, hold a full-time professional job and have insurance. When we talked to her a year following her graduation, she was starting her master's degree and concerned that her children have the correct educational credentials to be accepted by nationally recognized competitive universities. Zoe strived to thrive in a system that was foreign to her and in a system for which she was not prepared.

A classmate in her master's program is another marginalized student, Josie, who was afraid to speak to her advisor for two years. Although her college has a hold system, which requires that students see their advisors prior to registration, she managed to elude the system. Josie learned that she should not ask questions or seek out extra help. In her culture, only the majority students could do that. After almost being asked to leave college because she had failing grades, she finally answered a summons by her associate dean. Following the meeting with her associate dean, Josie and her advisor developed a plan for her to receive academic and study support. Her advisor also planned a schedule for her that helped her manage her course work.

Ferris State University (FSU) implemented academic support sections, the Structured Learning Assistance program referred to in the previous chapter. Specifically, the university identified specific classes where students typically had trouble, such as introductory-level mathematics, English, sociology, and psychology. It then designed a support system, involving faculty working with academic support personnel to identify key learning objectives, concepts, strategies, and skills, which are important to the course. Following each class section, there are parallel sections that the students attend to receive additional instruction from the support personnel. Tony, who we met in an earlier chapter, attended the academic support sections for some of his basic classes. Although he still struggles and has to work very hard, he managed to make it to his senior year and will graduate from college.

According to the Thernstroms (2003), many African-American students take the lowest possible road to success and elect to compete at the most minimal level of challenge (p. 145). We find that many of our minority students do not know that they are competing at low levels. Specifically, they do not know that a D or D- is not passing. Recently, some instructors at FSU drew bold lines under the letter grade C in their syllabi to demonstrate visually that anything below that line is considered not passing and that in college grades all grades must be above the line. On the other hand, some black students will strive for only B's and C's, because the are afraid of their black friends criticizing them for acting "white" if they were to get high grades (McWhorter, 2003, p. 154).

Mosley (2000) writes about how African-Americans have been marginalized for a long time in this country and that many of our social ills have been portrayed as minority issues. Because this process has been going on for a long time, he believes that blacks see themselves as victims of injustice. However, his view of victimization crosses all marginalized people, not just blacks. Many marginalized students enter academe with an invisible "V" for victim painted on their foreheads and embedded in their brains. Their behavior is often self-defeating and leads them to failure, not success. They will say that they do not understand it so they will not read it. Recently, while giving an oral report, a minority female switched from academic discourse to a ghetto-type language. Her classmates chastised her for hiding behind the "jive talk" because she was not prepared. Similarly, a young man from a rural community, recently, told self-deprecating jokes in a class discussion, rather than engage in academic discourse. Often students use their lack of knowledge or ill-preparation by acting as victims. When this behavior results in failure and dismissal from college, they self-confirm their victimization.

In an earlier chapter, we described the partnership between FSU and Bay Mills Community College. The latter, a tribal college, provides a teacher education certification program for Native-Americans who will ultimately teach in schools enrolling Native-American students. The partnership is in its third year and educating its third cohort of teaching candidates. Although the class is small—under 20 students—the partners view this collaboration as successful because its graduates are succeeding as teachers. Additionally, more programs are emerging from the partnership. These new programs give more Native-American students access to higher education; an access heretofore denied.

In Wolverine, Michigan, a small, rural school district where more than half of the students qualify for free or reduced lunches, dropout rates are historically high, and achievement tests results indicate that many students have difficulty learning. Recently, the new superintendent developed a partnership with a community college to dual enroll some of its juniors and seniors. As the students started taking classes at the community college, achievement scores went up and dropout rates went down. The students began to see the world beyond their community and develop aspirations heretofore unattained.

Maxine Greene (1988) argued throughout her career at Teachers College that advising students actually meant helping them find their voices and a public space to stand in. She wrote: "The matter of freedom ...in a diverse society is also a matter of power, and it involves the issue of public space (p. 116)." Finding a space for oneself is finding out who we are in relation to others and the world. To find one's space requires participation in the political sphere in the broadest sense of that idea. Only then can individuals find themselves in the midst of peers. Greene says that the principal obstacle to students gaining self-respect is the "lack of mutuality and care (Ibid.)." So, we believe what is missing in the school and university advisors' role is the personal care for the individual student's success. This requires personal connections between advisor and advisee and that is a scary prospect for many in the school counseling business. But, when the proposition is put in terms of freedom and the obstacles to its realization in the lives of marginalized students, excuses are lame at best. The very purpose of obstacles is to be overcome. Again, Greene writes, "The point is not that there are never any excuses, it is that, in classrooms as well as in the open world, accommodations come too easily (p. 5)."

Abigail and Stephan Thernstrom (2003) tell us that there are a few "terrific schools that serve highly disadvantaged minority kids," (p. 4), but there are not as many as needed. These few schools operate on the premise that there are "no excuses" for failure. "Every student is expected to work hard to acquire the skills and knowledge that tests measure (Ibid.)." Nevertheless, the obstacles preventing such schools becoming the norm in America are huge. And, at the base of these obstacles, is the bedrock of underfunding of our schools. The money is not there in our current economy and it is beginning to look worse for our future funding of education. Until that level of money arrives, which may be never, is there not something educators can do? The answer is a very positive, "Of course!" Bob Herbert, the *New York Times* columnist (2003), acknowledges that there are many hard-working teachers, who even pay for extra supplies when needed and are available to students in trouble. However, "there are many, many others who are not remotely interested in these kids. They tell the kids to their faces: 'I don't care what you do. I'm still going to get paid (p. A23)." Teachers, who would blame the parents for students' failure to perform, communicate those expectations to their classes. There is little talk of working hard, burning the midnight oil, and finding the help students need to succeed academically. Just as it is all too easy for teachers to blame the parents, so too, it is all too easy for critics to blame the teachers for students' failures in school.

Recent studies of why teachers stay in the profession of teaching (Johnson & Birkeland, Fall, 2003) confirm our argument that administrative and collegial support for teachers make a difference in creating positive professional aspirations. Johnson & Birkeland did interviews with 50 new teachers over their first three years of teaching. They found that teachers who felt that their school supported them in their teaching, "providing collegial interaction, opportunities for growth, appropriate assignments, adequate resources, and schoolwide structures supporting student learning—were more likely to stay in their schools... (p. 581)." Why not give teachers every chance to succeed in their careers? There is much that can be done to assure quality leadership in the next generation of teachers. Not offering the initial support to new teachers is just plain sloppy educational administration.

Much of the problem of sloppy and ineffective schooling can be laid at the feet of racism in America. McWhorter (2003) argues that racial profiling "is not just one problem on the landscape of race relations—it is the main thing distracting African-Americans from sensing themselves as true Americans rather than a 'people apart.' (p. 38)." If society at large does not care about the marginalized citizens of the country, is it any wonder that such attitudes invade our schools? Matching racism as an obstacle to school reform is the other side of the coin, so to speak; what McWhorter calls "the cult of Victimology." Blacks match whites' negative expectations with their own self-defeatist attitudes. Furthermore, McWhorter describes a "cult of Separationism" in which African-Americans are "subject to looser standards of judgment." And finally, McWhorter says racial profiling includes a "cult of Anti-Intellectualism (p. 39)." Society has mostly low expectations regarding the scholastic performance of African-Americans—and this thinking is pervasive even within the black community. There is the sense that nothing can be done to change their fate so they might as well accept their roles as victims, separate people, and anti-intellectuals. We can see this working out in the lives of African-American high-school students who did relatively well in primary school, but when faced with the demands of middle and high-school curricula, turn away in disgust and self-loathing.

Continuing McWhorter's (2003) argument, he sees little change in these attitudes toward education very soon in our history. "Overall," he writes, "the black educational establishment is focused more on decrying why black children *cannot* learn than how they *will* learn (p. 51, emphasis in the original). Meanwhile, our society as a whole must search for curricular approaches to the problems of marginality in our schools and colleges without caving into racial profiling. There may be much that African-Americans must get over in the history of their treatment in America, so, too, there is much that the non-black community can get over in its assumptions about the African-American community and its characteristics. A place to start for improvement is to cut out the racial, gender and ethnic profiling that goes on in schools and universities. Eliminate standardized and shopworn truisms about what people are "supposed to be." Write a curriculum with powerful expectations for everyone. The discipline we expect from individuals to succeed in schools must first be practiced by the educational establishment. Do you want motivated students who burn the midnight oil? Then let's see some motivated educators, burning the midnight oil to write relevant curricula for their students, grade every paper for every assignment and communicate their judgments on student performance with grace and sensitivity. What we expect of others, we must first expect of ourselves!

What we are promoting here are not special standards for marginalized students, but higher standards for all of our students. McWhorter (2003) makes this point nicely in reference to the political arena. He chastises the Democratic Party as captivated by the pleas of identity politics; that is, the belief that African-Americans "are piteous souls incapable of achieving without handouts." He continues, "To condition a people to handouts is to disempower them (p. 60)." Special treatment has always had the underside of lowered expectations and unchallenged minds, no matter whether the recipients are majority or marginal students. Whenever someone gets a "free ride" in academia, that person pays the price later on for not accomplishing the best he or she can do. Mark Edmundson (2002) reminds us that "the great teacher is not always a bringer of sweetness and light (p. 11)." Great teachers more characteristically demand our highest commitment, the most that we can give to our studies. We remember a great professor in graduate school who said in a class we took on ancient Middle-Eastern history and thought; "You cannot understand the Semitic mind without knowing at least one of the languages in which these ancient documents are written." He argued that, of course, we can always use translations to approximate meanings of ancient texts, but that nothing surpasses the functional familiarity with the language itself. Although we were close to finishing a doctorate and we had family responsibilities, we decided nothing would do but to take another year and study Hebrew to "get inside" the early biblical texts. It was hard. But that professor was right; we found a way to survive, and when we did we discovered that we were thriving in the midst of riches of insight we did not know were there or even possible. Yes, great teachers are often our toughest critics because they have seen with their own eyes a vision of where the mind can take us.

The myth of the infinitely kind and benevolent teacher is exposed by Edmundson. Nonetheless, we are not selling meanness as an effective teaching strategy. Sympathy and empathy are always relevant to the classroom, especially for students feeling like outsiders to the system and who do not have much appreciation for their own stature and heritage. Teaching is easy enough if you have no professional standards, want to leave school by 3 p.m., and take a three month vacation every summer. But, if you care for your students and your subjects as a teacher, it is a tough profession. It takes years to become a good teacher and it takes a lifetime to become a great teacher. Rafe Esquith (2003) describes his own journey from a new, inexperienced teacher to becoming a first-rate teacher. "It was fabulous being a young male teacher. I wasn't a very good one but was too ignorant to know it (p. 15)." Over the decades of teaching in what Esquith calls "the Jungle" of urban Los Angeles, he has learned that he has become a good teacher, maybe a great one. (In 1992, he received an Outstanding Teacher in America Award.) But he evaluates himself as a teacher by the accomplishments of his students. One of Esquith's students (named Matt) went on to become a lawyer and when he returned to Los Angeles, this young lawyer sought to help Esquith by incorporating his classroom, "making it permissible for me to raise funds for the children. (p. 203)." Esquith goes on to report how committed this busy lawyer is to helping his school. "Despite an eighty-hour work week, he constantly brings new patrons to the class who want to help deserving children. And Matt even takes me to Lakers' games occasionally when he worries that I'm working too hard (Ibid.)." He is right. If a teacher wants to know how good he or she is, look to the consequences; that is, keep track of students and what becomes of them.

School reform would be an easy proposition if we could magically transform every teacher into a Gatto or an Esquith. But the project of school reform is a corporate action with concrete institutional structures and policies. One person can make the decision to be a better teacher and commit to a program of hard work, passion and sensitivity to students and subjects taught. But we cannot find the means to create incentives for such decisions in the lives of teachers nor find the tools of commanding extraordinary commitment of all teachers. In fact, most teachers work very hard and are exhausted at the end of the day for the struggle to achieve anything more than survival. The issues of school reform, therefore, remain issues of corporate reconstruction. The community must take action. The school district must lead and find the resources to afford the leadership needed to reform the educational profile of the district. Likewise, the action must reach out to all educators at all levels of the educational spectrum. We have been arguing that collaboration among educators and institutions of learning is the only vehicle of hope if school reform will succeed in bringing justice and fairness to the possibilities of educational achievement.

Community colleges now have another role added to their higher education services. Since the No Child Left Behind (NCLB) legislation and rulings by the Secretary of Education, students who do not pass a standard test are often denied a high school diploma. Many school districts are not equipped nor funded to offer make up courses for such students and, to the eyes of the administration, these students had their chance to earn a diploma and blew it. The local community colleges are trying to figure out how to serve these students because they already provide remedial education to college students. Dean and Provost Newsletter (2003), reports that "colleges in some states have stepped up and helped. In Massachusetts (MA), colleges established a program to get students up to speed and get their high-school diploma (p. 4)." The approach may be necessary if these students are to qualify for financial aid. Currently, they may not receive financial aid without proving their ability to benefit from a college education. Taking on this role and filling in the gap in educational practice was not designed by some rational national policy, but fell to the community colleges by default. Who else is left to care for these students who finish high school without earning a diploma? The Department of Education just assumes that local educational agencies will pick up the pieces of their policy accidents. Even as they make such assumptions, they require that local school districts use their Title I funds to pay for alternative providers of tutors and learning centers. There remains lots of money to be payed to reading clinics and tutoring businesses. No wonder that Sylvan Learning Centers lobbied heavily for this regulation!

At the college level change is difficult admittedly; and one of the major factors is the faculty's resistance to change. Student's are also incredibly loyal to the lecture system of instruction. Benvenuto (2002) has written about why the traditional lecture continues to be the pedagogical choice in higher education, even in the face of evidence to contrary that other forms of learning are more effective (p. 65). He lists several reasons for the popularity of the lecture: for example, students seem more comfortable with lectures (perhaps because they can hide in the large classrooms and not be accountable); also, students report consistently that they read assignments after lectures so that they can study only the essential material addressed in the lecture; students also see the lecture as a commodity they have paid for, as a something they have bought and are entitled to, even if in the form of friends' notes on the lecture (pp. 65-69). On the faculty side, instructors feel that their lectures are working just fine for them; and further they find it difficult to imagine how to evaluate the quality of other teaching methodologies (pp. 70-71).

Lee Shulman offers a "different way to think about accountability" among the faculty. He writes in a series of short commentary on higher education reform called the *Carnegie Foundation Perspectives* (October 2003). He points out that faculty accountability for the consequences of their teaching extends beyond the matter of fact addressing of traditional methods of lecturing and examinations. He asks, "Do we need teachers who see student learning and its improvement as their professional, ethical responsibility? Absolutely." Shulman tells how many faculty "go beyond the call of duty" and take on students who need special help to learn their assignments. He argues that such actions are not "beyond the call of duty," but precisely what is required. "Teachers must accept the ethical as well as the intellectual and pedagogical challenges of their work." If he is right, and we believe he is on the right track, then higher education faculty must take on a much broader range of responsibility for the conditions and outcomes of student learning.

The continuing discrimination in America in all of our institutions is the cause for rededication to reform. Brown, et al. (2003), writes about "whitewashing race" or, as they call it, "the myth of a color-blind society." Their main point is that the gains in racial equity made in the 1960s and 1970s have ceased to be matched and, in fact, there is some evidence of reversal. "Today optimism about the future of racial justice has been swapped for fatalism and a sense of possibility stymied by what passes for necessity and 'realism.' (p. vii)." Talk about creating a color-blind society appears to be a sham hiding, instead, a very *color-conscious* notion (p. 197)." Throughout our discussions of the crisis in the American dream of education in a just society, we have pointed to the nearly one-third of the school population that is treated unfairly as marginalized students. Racism and gender and class bias continue to haunt the organization, administration and instructional programs of our schools and colleges. No Child Left Behind has created new unintended consequences by increasing, rather than decreasing the "graduation rate gap" between whites and persons of color (see: "Special Issue on Accountability and Equity" AERJ, 2004). Rather than making progress, we indeed have evidence that newly established national standards in student testing and curricular demands on schools have created greater frustrations and demands on students and teachers alike.

Whether we focus on race or gender or class, the charges of neglect and animosity can be sustained by the evidence. African-American students are failing to graduate from high school in greater percentages than ever before since Florida mandated artificial testing standards for diplomas. Female discrimination continues in jobs, especially in pay, even among school administrators. Blue-collar workers' children feel like outcasts in our schools and colleges; they feel they don't fit in and will never fit in with the easygoing high- and middle-class bosses (Lubrano, 2003). All of these categories of discrimination perpetrate a sense of isolation among those feeling like outcasts. It is not merely a matter of the denial of material wealth that hurts the marginalized, rather "it has to do with learning and possessing confidence in your place in the world (Lubrano, 2003, p. 9)." Working-class women are especially cramped by family expectations. Women who compete on the career market are often cautioned by family members that they would be taking a job from a man "who has a family to feed." Some working-class families have expectations for their female children that are very specific. Lubrano tells of an award winning African-American/Latino journalist whose mother's plans for her were to work in a department store at a cosmetics counter. The mother was disappointed with her daughter's career choice and, to this day, never celebrates her daughter's successes (see, p. 35).

One of the reasons that minorities feel marginalized or like outsiders when they come to a college campus is that they have such little contact with whites in their schools and urban communities. Thernstrom & Thernstrom (2003) write about the increasing racial isolation in America. They refer to the work of Gary Orfield, who created an "Index of Exposure," which shows the decline in the proportion of whites enrolled in predominately minority schools. Orfield's data show that minority exposure to whites has been declining since 1986. "In Orfield's view, black, Hispanic, Asian, and American-Indian students all belong to one undifferentiated "minority" group, and that group is "segregated" because the youngsters who belong to it are exposed to too few whites (p. 175)."

The isolation of minorities from whites as a fact explains, to some extent, the trauma Lubrano (2003) describes that minorities experience when they go to universities. There is an "us versus them" aura when minorities experience middle-class and upper-class students on a college campus. Lubrano says that when he went to Columbia University he had never seen anyone dress like the students he saw there and so he felt out of place (p. 74). To make it worse, Lubrano could find no one with whom he could talk about his day in college at home in Brooklyn. One of our colleagues reports that in the class he is teaching, there is an African-American female student from Detroit whose family is very well connected politically in Michigan. Nevertheless, in his class, she jive talks in Ebonics and wears gang/ghetto clothes. A black male student in the class asked to speak with this instructor after class and he apologized for her language, behavior, and dress. This student said that her family would be embarrassed if they know she was using such language and behavior. Then he said: "I guess you can take the girl out of the ghetto, but not the ghetto out of the girl." The dislocation a minority student feels upon first encounter with the college environment is part of the result of isolation from whites during the high-school experience.

The tensions remain even in the midst of efforts for orientation and accommodations in our entry programs. A major factor, of course, in the continuing struggle with life on the margins is the continuing reality of racial inequality today. Brown and his associates (2003) recognize that many of the policies and programs that are proposed to deal with injustice in our educational system "are universalistic in that they benefit disadvantaged people of all races (p. 231)." Still, we agree with Brown et al., that such universalistic or even class-based policies by themselves will not remedy the injustices and isolations experienced by marginalized students. They write, "...[w]e see no point in proposing universalistic policies that reinforce racial inequalities. The best policies mitigate racial inequality while also, if possible, lifting all boats. The minimum wage is an example, since it benefits low-income workers of all races (Ibid.)."

We have been arguing the case for educational reform through the creation of new communities of collaboration among institutions, from K-12 school systems to graduate universities. At all levels the attention to the needs of marginalized students will, in effect, create the conditions for the improvement of all the standards for education. We believe that inventing procedures and practices that mitigate racial inequity does not mean that something has to be taken away from some group of citizens to create more justice. Contrary to popular opinion, knowledge is not limited in quantity or restricted to a finite collection of facts, no matter how meaningful. Learning is an open and on-going process that invites more and more learners to participate. Again, Peter Brook taught us in his book *The Open Door*, that there are no secrets. Knowledge keeps growing and sound educational policy promotes the exploration of where new knowledge is taking the human race, irrespective of race, gender or class.

Issues and Questions for Chapter Seven

Exploring the Struggle to Succeed

- Success in the academic world is an issue of achievement. Gaining understandings of self and the world requires the particular sharing of resources with others.
- Academic fortitude comes with the acquiring a commitment to learn in context.
- This kind of commitment can "shake off the dead hand of history (see Mosley, 2000)."
- "Blacks have historically been marginalized and many social ills have been presented as minority issues."
- But, denied access may be the result of economic constraints brought on by class position, the issues are not confined to minority groups.
- Teaching people of all social groups how to cope with the complexities of a contemporary education is more than focusing on minority issues.
- Denied access to universities is a problem that cuts across ethnic, racial, religious, regional backgrounds. It is a multicultural problem and a multicultural response is called for. So, the colleges and universities will have to change as well

Global Community Groups

- How can looking beyond the local knowledge base help us to connect with global issues without discarding the pivotal value of local knowledge?
- One clue is that creating space for change to happen

may require global connected locations to gather and to share.

- Critical dialogue opens up new ideas and we need new ideas if we are to change.
- By risking a trial of new activities aimed at helping students develop academic fortitude we may very well be reforming schools and colleges for this new century.

Emerson and the Party of Hope

- Emerson distinguished between the party of memory and the party of hope.
- Cynics join the party of memory and cite history to show that dreams for improving America are impossible.
- When cynics describe America as an empire, it can lead students to give up their parents' hope in reformist politics to cope with injustice.
- The worst thing when faced with failure and frustration is to do nothing.
- Hope is the exercise of our humane center, that life can be better for all.
- To win, nobody else has to lose. To succeed, nobody else has to fail. To gain knowledge is to contribute to the social pool of understandings and everyone gains!
- Schools and universities must be linked to assure equal access to education in America, as we have yet to reach out fairly to all the citizens and residents of this beautiful country.

"The scholar finds certainty in the heart.
The world may be studied from a book.
A classroom may be a universe.
All we experience is first hand.
The more we travel,
The harder it is to understand.
Not understanding is:
The beginning of wisdom."
No. 47, *The Tao of Teaching*

CHAPTER EIGHT
Dumbing Down School Curricula

Policy promoting the belief that a marketplace economy is the last court of appeals in America has infested the No Child Left Behind curricula. By reducing everything to a bottom-line accountability, we oversimplify our complex world, especially how diverse populations of students learn. This tendency is labeled "21st Century Philistinism" by Frank Furedi and represents, he thinks, grounds for a new cultural war. Schools and the curricula offered in them are more and more crafted into exercises in rote learning and narrowly constructed morality simplifications. What is true is portrayed as black and white realities, which parallels the national policy of a world split into friends and enemies. We are told that empires of evil exist terrorizing our future survival. So, simple tests of support or opposition are offered to explain the world. The danger this generates can be witnessed by schools offering curricula over-simplified into superficial either/or realities. Classes are arranged in 45-minute segments. Lessons are organized around simple objective right versus wrong constructions. Tests measure multiple choices to find the seemingly right answer. The impact of such simplicities is especially felt in urban and isolated rural communities. Mathematics, for example, is simply not taught to African-Americans or northern American Indians past the sixth grade. By the time of high school, students either know how to read or they are not taught to read. By high school, students either know how algebra works as a tool for understanding or students are dumped into dumbed down classes of general math. Attention to the learning needs of individual students and groups of students is ignored in a simplified world of No Child Left Behind school curricula. Finally, national policy rewards those schools whose students already have mastered the basics of reading and mathematics, while schools that have been ignored in funding, leadership and social capital have funds withdrawn as punishment for not achieving national goals.

We live in a complex and real world; to make all problems and issues we face into simple pro/con, right/wrong, yes/no is an exercise in triviality at best and stupid at worse. One of the more prominent arenas where this mindlessness is found is in the current debates about public school curricula, which seem to mimic the simplicities that characterize our national political discourse. Accountability testing, for example, seems driven by the impulse to simplify knowledge and reduce understanding to an exercise in rote constructions. America is in danger of becoming a more narrow, moralistic and simple-minded society. As education reflects the nation's culture, what we struggle with nationally and internationally has all the appearance of efforts to "dumb down" our fundamental problems into superficial either/or realities. By using the term "dumb down" we refer not to people or are represented as "dumb," but to intentional policies which seek to simplify school curricula.

This national crisis is most clear in how we, as a nation, present ourselves to the world. We were confronted with our national image on a trip to Asia recently. We took a taxi in downtown Bangkok and the taxi driver, a self employed Thai businessman, asked if we were American. We said, "Yes, we are." He said that he was angry at President Bush for turning the world into two camps—pro-America or anti-America—with his suggestion that those countries "against" the war in Iraq were our enemies. The taxi driver said, "After all the years we have been America's best friend in Southeast Asia, all of a sudden we are supposed to be either a friend or an enemy, depending whether we support the Bush war on Iraq." Speaking clearly in English and expressing this complex thought, the taxi driver shared with us his frustrations with America. People around the world are not stupid. They can express their dismay at America seemingly driving the world into competing camps. They experience the "dumbing down" of American foreign policy and they resent it.

The problem in American schools is complex and not merely a problem with instruction, nor a shortage of smart teachers and administrators, nor better textbooks, nor higher pay and better-quality building facilities; it is also a basic problem with the structure of American schools. By structure, we mean the issues as to who is in charge, where the money comes from, what the essential goals of education are, and how educators make choices and decide on appropriate courses of action. If more and more decisions about schooling and the curricula are made by people who have less and less a personal and vital interest in the consequences of those decisions, than the structure of education is flawed. If we reward schools who succeed with bonus money, we take away funds from those very schools which need the most funding. If the goals of education are set by national agenda and prescribed by accountability schemes, then local commitment to an educational mission is lessened. And, if more and more time in classrooms is spent on mandated programs from state and national politicians, professional teachers will feel marginalized and lose respect for their work. The links between structural effectiveness and school curricula become apparent under examination.

Waiting to teach some students how to read until the 9th grade is dumbing down the high-school curriculum. Ignoring mathematics beyond simple arithmetic until middle school is dumbing down middle-school curriculum. Focusing on problem-solving techniques will dumb down the social studies curriculum and deny students the opportunity to develop their own social capital. In brief, a yes/no curriculum design that explains everything as having simple right or wrong answers gives the major benefit to teachers by making it easier to write true/false quizzes and multiple-choice, one-right-answer questions. Making the stuff of life and our knowledge about the world into coherent formulas may be easier for teachers, but harder for their students in the long run. Eric Booth (2001) makes this point in his statement that "Reality is not simple, and representations that make it seem so are false...reading reality is a full-contact sport (p.214)."

Jacques Derrida was probably the most influential philosopher in the last half of the 20th century. His explorations into the hidden meanings of texts through deconstruction have been attacked from both the right and left of the political and religious spectrum. The religious right claimed Derrida represented a pagan nihilism that denied any support for moral certainty. The academic left attacked Derrida for his rejection of political correctness. Both sides misunderstood the serious search in Derrida's writings for moral purpose in human interaction. While denying that absolute values can be found, Derrida claimed one need not possess transparent truth in order to act with generosity and fairness toward one's fellow human beings. Mark Taylor (2004) wrote in a memorial essay that Derrida believed "true believers of every stripe— Muslim, Jewish, and Christian—...threaten to tear our world apart." The alternative to blind belief is a different kind of belief, Derrida claimed. It is a more rational, responsible and complex wisdom that seeks to help us respect those we do not understand. This new kind of belief is based on doubt and uncertainty, but it still provides a path for humane and just treatment of others. Tolerance for difference is based on tolerance for the complexities of our lives.

Yet we find public school curricula looking for easy solutions to easy problems. For example, some twenty years ago, we taught at the Michigan Allen Street School in Lansing, in its "Project Refuel." One of the tools we learned to use was how to implement an integrated math, English, social studies lesson in which the students were required to design dice. We visited the Educational Development Center in Newton, Massachusetts, in order to learn about how to teach that lesson. It was very complex, and we implemented it with seven-year-olds as a demonstration. Recently, we watched an Annenberg video on best teaching practices and it showed the use of a modification of that same lesson with fourth- and fifth-graders. Instead of pushing complex content down to younger grades, we are pushing it up. This reversal of the curriculum is what we mean by the "dumbing down" of curricula. Also, we find that a lesson popular with teachers will be taught over and over again at all grade levels. Often teachers of second-grade students are assigned to teach fifth grade. Guess what? They use much of the same lessons and strategies on the fifth-graders as they were familiar using with their second-graders. No wonder that students find the curricula simplistic, repetitive, and boring!

American students study dinosaurs repeatedly from kindergarten through fifth grade as well as Eskimos, penguins, and horses on the days that they are not studying for high-stakes tests. (However, we have heard of some school districts prohibiting the teaching about dinosaurs, because it is seen as part of the "evolution curriculum" sponsored by "Darwinians.") Students in China, however, are reading traditional literature and learning to place that literature in the contexts of past dynasties while European students are practicing multiple languages. One indicator of the dumbing down of our system is vocabulary. Few books introduce and utilize the critical vocabulary that students need to read complex texts and engage in deep discourse that leads to critical thinking.

In her studies of vocabulary acquisition, Sandra Stotsky (1997) found that elementary teachers often taught words with very limited utility, such as the Inuit term for "sunset," rather than more important terms that ensure future reading success and form the base of their academic vocabulary. As a caveat, we are not blaming teachers for teaching Inuit words to third-graders who will only use them once, but we do blame the textbook publishers and test constructors who send the message that by studying such content, students will pass tests. Yet, according to Stotsky, reading these texts have little impact on reading achievement because they have "few intellectual connections" to the readers and their culture (1997, 265). Stotsky contends that "a major goal of an instructional reader is to build up the children's ability to read—and use—literate English words (1997, 267)." Moreover, she suggests that having diminished opportunities to learn such words has dire consequences. Those consequences include students not being able to read and comprehend at age and grade-level expectations and "some publishers...choosing selections with an easier vocabulary than they might have otherwise chosen, in order to make [texts] more accessible to least able readers at each grade level (1997, 282)." And so it goes; the cycle continues by not providing the necessary vocabulary to support reading achievement and then choosing easier words to make future reading "accessible," resulting in all readers becoming less able.

Ellen Langer (1997) reminds us that students need multiple and different exposures to concepts as a means of developing meaningful learning. For example, simply looking at a pencil in different ways illustrates Langer's concept of meaningful learning. Specifically, holding it one way, the traditional way, it is a pencil. However, looking at a pencil from the top, it looks like a dot. Langer also suggests finding new uses for the concept. Not only can pencils be used for writing, they also can be used as bookmarks, doorstops, and window props. Students can find many other ways of looking at pencils and additional uses for pencils.

Unfortunately, too many teachers who are following prescriptive guides do not encourage their students to search for multiple meanings and alternative points of view. If multiple meanings of complex words are not taught early, students have difficulties learning various disciplines, making academic failure inevitable. A few years ago, we were in a middle school facilitating a workshop on literacy for the teachers. At the end of the day, we were asked to listen to an eighth-grader read because her reading baffled her teachers. After she read from her science book, she knew about waxing, but she did not know how to wax a moon let alone about "waning a moon." The experience with her social studies book was similar. She reported that she knew how to turn right, but not what it meant if "civil" was in front of it. As an eighth-grader with a woefully limited vocabulary, her prognosis for future academic success was limited. The tragedy is that in previous years, her teachers gave glowing reports about her reading and she performed satisfactorily on state-mandated tests. Passing along a student and ignoring liabilities is a form of dumbing down.

A fourth-grade teacher who brags about having high test scores also brags about teaching only skills. If she does, in fact, teach only skills, she will fall into the test trap and is dumbing down her students' futures. Since skills are contextual, teaching a "skills only" approach does not prepare students for the tools needed for the unknown future.

Recently, we heard Mary Catherine Bateson (2004) speak about an experience that she had as a young child when she was visiting her father, Gregory Bateson, a renowned scientist. At that time, Bateson was studying the learning capabilities of dolphins in Hawaii. If the dolphins caught a rubber ring and tossed it back to their trainers five times, the dolphins exhibited learning through stimulus-response methodologies. During the learning experiments, a graduate assistant pointed out that a particular dolphin did not seem to be able to learn. The dolphin in question never returned the ring to the graduate student more than four times. Instead, the dolphin repeatedly threw the ring aside, an action that required the graduate student to walk to an alternative location in order to retrieve the ring. When the graduate student reported the incident to

Bateson, she mentioned that the dolphin made a snickering sound. Bateson asked if she had recorded the behavior. The student's answer was no, explaining, in her defense that the recording form was not large enough. This is a story about academic dumbing down, because the graduate student had focused on a single behavior or an isolated specific learning outcome. When teachers focus on isolated behaviors, they miss an array of rich interactions and performances which may indicate advanced achievement. In this particular case, the dolphin had out-smarted the graduate assistant, even to the point of snickering at the handler.

A colleague was called to an urban high school to help the teachers improve students' reading acquisition skills. She found that many of the ninth-graders were reading at the fourth-grade level. Yet, instead of having reading instruction directed to elevating their reading comprehension, the teachers were having their students work on improving their self-concepts. The activity was a spin-off on the old song "Mother," as in "M is for the many things you gave me." These ninth-grade students were making posters using the letters of their first names to construct positive messages such as "Mary; M is for magnificent; A is for attractive; R is for righteous; and Y is for young." Now, let's remember that students are smart. They knew that they could not read as well as their peers. When they apply to enter college, will their self-concepts improve when they are rejected, principally because they cannot read?

Symptoms of dumbing down school curricula:

1. "Perpetuating the myth that America is a land of second chances." In fact, there are no second chances after failure in academia. "Try, try, and try again" does not make for progress, no matter how often the teacher repeats this shibboleth.

2. "Asserting that associates degrees are great." In fact, technical diplomas tend to slide the recipients onto a failure track.

3. "Purchasing textbooks from big publishing companies with their book deals will help educators focus on student achievement." In fact, textbook series provide material that rob teachers and students both from trusting their own cognitive powers by diverting them from teaching and learning and inviting them into rote recitations.

4. "Believing that the marketplace is the last court of appeals in America." In fact, reducing everything to "bottom-line" accountability, oversimplifies our complex world.

Deborah Meier (2002) characterizes most public schools as offering: "Dry textbooks and standardized curricula unconnected with any passions or interest of children, delivered by adults in seven, eight, or sometimes nine 45-minute time slots... (p. 12)" What is missing in the dumbing down curriculum is any genuine link with the adult world. The adult world is not experienced directly in schools; rather, it is offered as a virtual reality. The result is that students cannot trust their adult school teachers because the teachers pretend to be like children (many even speak in a child-like voice), which children recognize immediately as condescending and discounting. Meier (2002) urges the school curricula to be honest and engaging between students and their adult teachers. She writes that "greater, not less intimacy between the generations is at the heart of all the best school reform efforts around today and is the surest path to restoring public trust in public education." (p. 13)

Dorothy Shipps (Winter, 2003) has argued that reform is an unpredictable process heavy with political baggage. She writes that this may explain why the black-white performance gap remains large despite decades of reform. It may also explain "why children of low-income blacks have been disproportionately sanctioned... (p. 870)" Teachers are not urged to participate in any reform coalition, so reform is always starting a new "cycle of change."

Peter Schrag (2003) describes the "battle for adequacy in America's schools" and he believes that "...[the] adequacy argument is also a sophisticated and passionate declaration of faith in the great promises of American society: equality, opportunity, and human and social betterment-a *sine qua non* for a modem technological democracy." (p.248) In contrast, an inadequate, dumbed down curricula is a force against America's future. It cuts down on the access to employment in a technical economy and makes suspect the exercise of responsible citizenship.

The transition from adolescence to adulthood has been extended in American society, Mary Catherine Bateson (2000) argues, partially because of the complications involved with acquiring the understandings and skills needed to operate as adults, with all the responsibilities of citizenship, career and parenthood. Schools cannot be expected to do it all. She writes "that there is a need to acknowledge a life stage here with substance and social value, challenge and a sense of achievement, and to make it productive for both males and females." (p. 71)

One of the consequences of dumbing down school curricula is the minimalization of student learning. While minimalism is usually associated with an art movement, it can be seen as a consequential outcome of trimming school curricula. As a 20th-century art movement and style, it stressed the idea of reducing a work of art to the minimum number of colors, values, shapes, lines and textures. Minimal artists made no attempt to represent or symbolize any other object or experience. So, minimalism is sometimes called ABC art, minimal art, reductivism, and rejective art. Likewise, those who would limit school curricula to a focused group of goals that match standards of achievement accountability would clearly earn the descriptor of "minimalist." Through the use of various accountability schemes the temptation is huge to minimalize the range and scope of student effort and understanding. Peter Sacks (1999) reports that "one of the most damaging effects of large-scale, big-stakes standardized testing in schools has been to: (1) oversimplify what's taught in school; and (2) to severely constrict what is taught to only those items most likely to appear on the upcoming standardized test." (p. 128) So, our question remains: does a narrowing down approach to the curricula help ensure that students will become better communicators, engage in substantive discourse, or write more eloquently? The answer is: "No!" What it produces is a minimal performance.

Proposal A in Michigan changed the way local school operations are funded. (Arsen & Plank, November, 2003) However, it did not change the way schools funded infrastructure. Because Proposal A lowered property taxes to fund schools, it made voters less hostile toward bond issues for school buildings. "Michigan remains one of the few states that does not provide some form of subsidization for capital costs in low-property- wealth districts." (Ibid.) In fact, the property value of rich to poor districts in Michigan went from 5:1 to 50:1, which makes it possible for wealthy residential areas to build magnificent schools. The gap between wealthy school districts and poor school districts widened, even while Proposal A was providing state funds for operations. At the same time in Michigan the MEAP (Michigan Education Achievement Program) has contributed to the dumbing down of the school curricula, especially in the low-income school districts. If one combines the MEAP and accountability pressures which began in the late 1960s with Proposal A, Michigan became one of the worst states for minority education. Minorities in 12th grade are learning at the eighth-grade level of their white counterparts. School of choice has accelerated the decline. Some would argue that the evidence is strong enough to support thinking that this is an orchestrated decline. However, without engaging in serious conspiracy theory speculations, the hand of accountability testing does seem joined with the hand of fiscal control.

The struggle for control of the school curricula may be paralleled by the problems of financial morality among American business executives. It is laughable that conservatives complain about liberals fostering "class warfare" by focusing on the gap in educational and financial achievement that separate the rich from the poor. In fact, the conservatives invented class warfare and engage in it as standard practice in the business. For example, Wal-Mart, the world's largest retail business, has been investigated for ripping off its payroll workers by altering workers' timecards. The executives in Arkansas deny this is company policy. They can point to management guidelines that specifically reject altering time cards as a business practice. But their denial is histrionic! They say that all the companies in retail business do it, and at the same time they deny it, saying "it is against company policy to alter records." All the big retail players are doing it; that is, they are pushing profit on the backs of workers at the lowest-paid levels; workers who can barely pay their bills. The managers erase hours on time cards, thus cutting back on the pay due to workers. When interviewed by reporters, managers will deny any knowledge of time altering, except "off the record," when they complain that all of their regional managers push them to alter records. The big class warfare militia include Wal-Mart, Family Dollar, Toys "R" Us, Pep Boys, Kinkos, Taco Bell, and RentWays— only McDonald's seems to have adhered to the law in this regard. Wal-Mart managers who do not cooperate in keeping payroll costs down by erasing hours on time cards are fired. These companies are the very companies who are not satisfied with marginal profits of 5 to 10 percent; they want 35 percent profit on investments. What does this say about our national moral fiber? It seems as though such business executives are saying, "If you can gouge the poor and rob from the needy, do it!" The rule seems to be that the wealthy deserve to be even more wealthy." If moral caring does not matter any more, than everything that works is OK. In schools educators avoid the hard work it takes to teach significant and enduring subject matter; it is easier to teach the easy stuff, over and over, grade after grade. No wonder students get bored and then cannot succeed in colleges.

The parallels between dumbing down school curricula and the plethora of business frauds become clearer in the details; for example, look at the rise of the legal profession in America. Putnam (2000) describes the rapid expansion of the number of lawyers in America after 1970. In 1970 there was one lawyer for every 4.5 engineers and by the end of the century there was one lawyer for every 2.1 engineers. The class warfare, the riots, the "war on crime" in the last quarter of the 20th century led Americans to fear their fellow citizens. When we stopped trusting each other, we started going to our lawyers who advised us to "get it in writing." Putnam (2000, p. 147) quotes Marc Galenter as saying, "Lawyers contrive to provide 'artificial trust'…because lawyers are producers and vendors of impersonal cool trust."

We stopped trusting students in schools and universities and they stopped trusting their teachers. Maybe there were good reasons on both sides for trust to decline. Students may have taken on cheating as an educational standard and teachers may have engaged in vindictive punishments for the so-called disruptive child. The *Tao Te Ching* says: "He who does not trust enough will not be trusted." In academia nothing happens without trust. If we cannot trust our scientists to accurately report their data and draw warranted conclusions; if students think cheating on an exam or cribbing a paper is OK, as long as one does not get caught; and if our politicians consistently lie to the citizenry, then there is little hope for creating learning communities in schools. If a group does not commune, it learns not to trust. There once was a time when all an American business executive needed to close a deal was a handshake; now we need lawyers.

The dumbing down of school curricula in America is part of the process of the dumbing down of politics and economics to simpleminded axioms or problems. Murray Edelman (1988) taught us long ago to identify social and political problems by the authorship of the problem definer. "Problems come into discourse and therefore into existence as reinforcements of ideologies, not simply because they are there or because they are important for wellbeing." (p. 12) That is, we make up our problems out of the conditions in which we find ourselves, which are made up of our beliefs about ourselves and the world. So it is ideology that drives what we think we "discover" as a problem. What is a problem to some is a benefit to others, Edelman tells us (p. 14). As a result, the problem definer gets to give a name to a condition and the action to solve the problem is forged out of the benefits derived from the activity. For example, defining a problem as terrorism, may very well give the benefit of justifying a war one wants to wage. Edelman writes, "Such a bricolage of actions and language claims sometimes ameliorates the condition and sometimes makes it worse; but some consequences of the policies pursued are always inversions of the value formally proclaimed as the goal of the activity." (p. 16) Again, for example, one goes to war to bring about peace, as they say.

Considering Murray Edelman's analysis as a guide for understanding public policy like "No Child Left Behind;" it drives the actions that make education for marginalized students worse than it was before. One is advised to be suspicious of any government policy designed to solve a specific problem. Deep within the proposed course of action one will find the seeds of ambiguity and inversion of values. Education is not something that is done to people; rather it is something that happens within people. Defining someone a "slow learner" is a public policy decision that will guarantee the student will fail to learn.

Educators and policymakers are not the only ones who define problems. Students have their own way of defining the problems they face in their own terms. Dance (2002) explores why people classify blacks as inferior, in her book, *The Impact of Street Culture on Schooling.* She writes, "beneath the surface of tough postures lie student critiques of the schooling mechanisms that facilitate inequality (p. 3)." Black urban student behavior in classrooms can be understood as a form of political resistance to "Euro-assimilationist expectations (p. 37)." These students need competent teachers who respect them rather than disapprove of them. Such cultural challenges are not unique to the central urban schools; suburbia also suffers from dumbing down of expectations and disrespect of students.

Gaines (1998) writes about the "teenage wasteland," asserting that suburbia's children are basically the new "dead-end kids." No Child Left Behind legislation had promised to grapple with genuine problems of public education and the achievement gap. Yet the superficial effects of spelling out curriculum standards can be devastating. In Texas, for example, high-school teachers are required to teach "sentence fragments" because students are tested on their capacity to identify "sentence fragments." So, teachers end up avoiding literature in order to spend precious instructional time on bits and pieces of information that often have no reality base, except as a requirement on an achievement test. Sometimes the standards lead to misinformation being taught. In Texas, a teacher was teaching angles according to Texas standards and opened a book to demonstrate that the open book was flat, so it "was not really an angle." The students dutifully repeated the teacher's false declaration that "flat" meant no degrees. We seem to remember that there is such a reality as a straight angle with 180 degrees; and so, the miss-education of children goes on in the midst of assurances of "educational standards."

Deborah Meier (2002) asks us to exercise our imagination to grasp the extent to which we have been sold a bill of goods by the testing and standardization advocates. Not merely parents but also the teachers of our school children have been taught to suspend their judgment about their students' reading performance. She writes: "For a teacher who sees a kid day in and day out to admit that she won't know how well he reads until the test score arrives is not good news (p. 135)." In this sense, standardization is a form of dumbing down, not only the curricula, but also the professional judgment of the teacher. If a teacher is convinced that her professional judgment is not an adequate tool to measure learning progress, then the teacher is crippled as a professional. This is true, irrespective of whether the teacher's professional expectations get communicated to the student so that the student's learning matches the teacher's expectation.

The impulse for dumbing down the curriculum and substituting "standards" is reinforced often by state legislators, particularly in those states that have limited terms written into the state constitution (Michigan and Florida, for example). These legislators cannot look into the future and plan carefully for the long-run improvement of education. Rather, they want immediacy and positive results fast! They do not have the time to gain experience and understanding about public education, so they remain uninformed. Therefore, they talk of accountability, they look at the numbers, and they follow the latest media fads. At a recent Michigan American Council of Education (ACE) Network conference, the legislators who attended wanted to know the answers to such issues as completion rates, cost of technical programs, graduation rates, time that it takes to get a degree, post-graduation employment rates, and remedial rates, because there must be something wrong with high schools and colleges if they cannot attend to these "issues." Speaking at the conference on the final day, James Duderstadt (2004) spoke about quality education as a critical factor in a global economy. He made it clear that the new literacy was not the literacy of responding to facts, but the literacy of synthesizing new knowledge, namely, constructivism. Listening to Duderstadt, the legislators at the conference did not "get it."

What this says about the academic curriculum is that while the liberal arts are enjoying a renaissance in high schools and colleges, they are in political trouble. Those who hold on to the purse strings of public funds seek schools that will guarantee that their students will gain employability skills. Even in the rarified air of private universities, the liberal arts curricula are under suspicion. Parents who pay very large bills for private university tuition are pressuring the academy to provide "practical and employable content courses" as part of the liberal arts requirements. New York University has been experimenting with credit carrying practical courses in business management, accounting and summer internships in corporations, as part of a liberal arts major. Colgate University is also looking to the summer internship as an opportunity to expand the liberal arts students' experience with the intention of making them more employable. Or so it is said. Actually, the leaders of these liberal arts colleges believe that a liberal arts education leads to a greater ability to analyze data and human situations, come to constructive applications of such analysis, and transfer the results to a variety of usages. Yet, liberal arts colleges and universities feel the heat and need to respond to their clients who want something visibly practical and seemingly related to their children's employability.

Dumbing down the curricula also results from teacher specialization into subject areas and technical expertise. Darling-Hammond (1997) describes how many foreign school teachers stay with their students over several years. (p. 135) In Japan, for instance, the teacher keeps the same students for two years. The first year is a "get to know them year." In the second year, the real learning goes further and deeper as teachers and students learn to respect and trust each other. Likewise, in German schools some teachers keep their students over several years and see their roles as also counselors and coaches. If teachers do not have such special long-term contact with their students, the cafeteria-style of organizing the curriculum becomes the norm. Teachers see themselves as a "math teacher" or "chemistry teacher" not as a counselor or even a language arts teacher. One result of over-specialization of the professional staff is that the students feel isolated from the teachers and teachers see themselves as teaching subjects rather than helping students develop over time. Schools that are organized as learning communities focus on the learning and less so the informing of facts. The students are at the center of the enterprise and not the lecturing nor the disciplining. Where student learning is the focus in a classroom, discipline rarely is a problem. But a school organized into specializations and modularizations is in the process of dumbing down the curriculum.

John Taylor Gatto (2002) in his wonderful book, *Dumbing Us Down,* writes about the importance of local control of schools and compares schools with the Congregational churches of New England, where "local skills, local knowledge, local love, local fidelity..." (p. 80) dominated the community culture. A school run from a distance by a central administrator under the direction of state and national government mandates is not much of a community; it is much more like a franchise. A franchise tries to serve up the same fare daily whatever the location. But the curriculum made over into a franchise of a state mandated menu is clearly pegged at the lowest common denominator; and that is what dumbing down the curriculum is all about.

When the curriculum of a school is dumbed down, those students most affected are those with the least resources to cope with the consequences, namely those students at the margins, especially African-Americans. Loury (2002) has argued that racial stigma is an important factor in African-American self-image. When low expectations of African-Americans is matched by over-simplified, dumbed down lessons, the consequences are devastating on academic achievement, especially in the first years of post-secondary education. The failure rate of marginalized students is higher and their academic fortitude is thin.

Thernstrom and Thernstrom (2003) show a 12-point difference between African-American performance on quantitative tests taken at the 12th-grade level and compared with white students' scores at the 8th-grade level. (p. 276) Throughout elementary school the minority students score at about the same rates as the white students. What happens after the seventh grade to support this significant difference in academic quantitative learning favoring white students over African-American students? African-American students are systematically assigned to non-algebraic mathematics courses. Their curriculum is dumbed down. By the time the African-American students enter college, they cannot compete. The Thernstroms (2003) tell the story: "Approximately two-thirds of black and Hispanic do not enter the workplace immediately, but go on to college, and a great many are clearly entering higher education unprepared for true college-level work." (p. 15) Even those African-Americans who survive the college-level work experience, do not, as a rule, choose to go into a research academic field, because of low achievement scores in mathematics. This seems to be true even of African-Americans who succeed in attending elite higher education institutions. (Cole and Barber, 2003, p. 99)

Why the racial achievement gap widens so dramatically between 8th grade and 12th grade is a difficult question to answer. Certainly, there may not be a simple single answer. However, one can identify several factors that may contribute to this achievement gap. One factor is the quality of teachers teaching in inner city schools. As long as the mathematical knowledge required of teachers focuses on arithmetic and numbering, most teachers can teach students successfully. Somewhere between 6th and 8th grade, algebraic concepts begin to appear in the required lessons. Competent teachers at this level of mathematics get thinner. By the time students enter high school, mathematics teaching requires special training and experience. So, there are fewer qualified mathematics teachers at the secondary school level. In the competition for staff, the better funded schools have an edge. So, inner city schools do not attract fully competent mathematics teachers. Another factor to consider in the racial achievement gap is the teacher expectations of African-American students as needing lower-level mathematics instruction. African-American students are often assigned to review mathematics courses, such as "pre-algebra." In such courses, all the elementary mathematics and arithmetic concepts are reviewed again and again. The consequences are devastating. Students get bored and begin to believe that they must be dumb to have to go over stuff they have already learned. So, the stage is set for widening the gap between white students and minority students in high school.

The gap that we are discussing here, let us remember, is an achievement gap, not an ability gap. So, once again we find ourselves dealing with the reality of racism in American education. The evidence is clear. Something happens to minority children in the middle of their schooling. African-Americans are treated as if they are slow, unimaginative, dangerous and lacking self-motivation. If one is so treated, so one responds; the actions of marginalized children seek out to fulfill what is expected of them. They become less successful. The test scores demonstrate the widening achievement gap between whites and blacks over the high school years.

Americans are being sold a bill of goods on the value of testing. We are told that achievement tests measure something real, like taking a person's temperature with a thermometer. The thermometer is an instrument of testing that measures something real happening inside a person's body and reports the temperature to the reader of the instrument. The consistency of the measuring device over time, location and among populations makes the information it reports trustworthy. The makers of education achievement tests would have us believe that their tests actually measure merit in the performance of the test-takers. It is a huge business, test-making and scoring and analyzing, and the enterprise makes lots of money for lots of people. But if the tests themselves are biased with racist assumptions, what good are they but to advance racist discrimination against students marginalized by the school systems offering the tests? The lie is in the presumptions of innocence on the part of the test-makers. "We are just asking questions!" We are forced to ask who benefits from the entire enterprise? The most obvious answer is the testing industry. The second most obvious answer as to who benefits is a racist school system that consistently, year after year, discriminates against minority students by both the instruction and the testing.

However, these data do not deny the fact some minority students do quite well on the tests and succeed in schools and universities. They gained academic fortitude in some manner through their families, friends, churches, schools and communities. We know minorities have the ability to achieve academically. The question is why don't they succeed in the same proportions as the rest of population? The list of answers is long:

1.   Money: minority schools receive less financial support than white suburban schools;

2.   Social support: inner city environments lack in security, services, and sustainability when compared with suburban communities;

3.   Building maintenance: the quality of many of the school buildings are under-cared for when contrasted to the new and shinny schools of suburbia;

4.   The teachers tend to be less qualified in urban schools than in suburban schools;

5.   Parental engagement urban schools is very low compared with the huge support of the PTA in majority community schools. There are more single-parent homes in the inner city than in the suburbs, and there are those who would blame the victims of living in such conditions generation after generation and not pulling themselves up by their boot straps and "make something of themselves."

This is racism. National leadership is steeped in the unction of racist intentions; if one were to measure that leadership in the NCLB program by the consequences of the program. What is created in the testing empires is a procedure that discriminates against a minority and marginalized population of students. They count on the country believing in the big lie: namely, if you work hard, so the promise goes, No Child Will Be Left Behind. The implication is clear: if you fail, you haven't worked hard enough. So, a course of goals over the next decade is set. If schools fail to meet these ever higher standards of achievement on the tests, money will be taken away; fewer incentives for improvement will be provided, and eventually schools may be closed or taken over by central agencies. In the meantime, those who suffer the most are the students themselves. Self-loathing prompted by failures reported in test scores does not lead to productive encouragement toward citizenship and acceptable, self-sustaining employment. As a result, the dream of achievement through education is systematically denied.

Some estimate that American students at all levels take nearly 400 million standardized tests per year. (Sacks, 1999) Add to that another 200 million tests taken in the rest of the American enterprises, including military, business and psychological, and the result is that Americans take 600 million tests per year—or nearly two tests per person in the country. As a culture we have been convinced that these tests tell us something important about ourselves, and just what that is can be analyzed by various experts interpreting the tests. Test results are believed to provide labels for who we are, and supposedly, how we are doing compared with the rest of the population. However, a test-oriented culture makes the mistake of assuming some kind of authenticity is represented by the tests we take. We do not say that these tests do not mean something, but they might not represent realities about what we know and what we can do. Eagleton (2004) reminds us that just because there are different answers to different questions, does not mean that we cannot distinguish between true and false statements. We must, however, recognize that there are questions that yield useful answers about the world and questions that lead us back to the question poser. In the case of educational testing, and maybe in all psychological testing, the questions are asked by specialists who define how they think the world *should* be. That is, they have a theory about the human beings are take their tests and how we should be labeled, sorted and promoted or denied. To believe this special theory about the world is to believe that test writers know something the rest of us do not know. That belief is very tenuous indeed.

Such thinking about tests and their value to our society might not be so harmful if it was merely a debate engaged in by scholars and academics. That is not the case. Believing in tests and the results they purport to provide us is harmful to our society in many ways, but most harmful to those who accept these labels that place them at the bottom of some magical scale, like the ability curve. Once students believe that they belong in the back of the classroom, all is lost for them in attaining any academic fortitude that might have provided the incentive to work hard and do well. Giving up on oneself because one believes in test labels, like slow leaner, is to deny personal knowledge about self and to turn one's life over to someone else's opinion. It is the road to injustice, fueled by racism and the belief in meritocracy instead of democracy.

Standardized testing serves more of a gate-keeping function than to provide authentic performance assessment. Because standardized tests seek to assess every student, in every location in definable levels of learning, it does have the consequences of dumbing down the school curricula. The "one size fits all" approach to standardized testing cannot but compel the curricula taught in schools to be uniform and non-local in detail. For example, as test makers try to measure student writing development, there is a strong temptation to use multiple-choice and short-answer questions so that the teachers will, in turn, focus instruction on language arts elements that can be squeezed into such subjects as punctuation, spelling and the mechanics of grammar. It is not that students should not learn grammar; rather, the place to learn it is in the writing itself. Instead of formulistic three-point paragraphs, teachers can encourage students to widen the scope of their writing in both research writing and creative writing. Of course, this would compel teachers to read the deeper and more complicated essays and provide feedback to students individually. That is what makes for authentic assessment; namely, teachers working with students on the development of their writing and expression skills. Such a curriculum would not be a dumbed down grab-bag of grammar and punctuation, but a smartened-up reach for student advanced achievement. Some of the more interesting and effective schools conceive of their curricula as organized in learning communities and they assess learning by more authentic processes, including student portfolios. Portfolio assessment requires local community involvement in the schools and, therefore, the realities of the local community enter into the curriculum and become major assets for student learning.

A community school is precisely a place where students feel that they belong. It is a place that takes the time to care about individual students by getting to know who they are and what they can do. The talk among teachers in community schools is about individual students: William, Ruth, Sam and Julie. A place where I belong knows my name; I feel at home there and I am eager to take on my role in the community and embrace the responsibility citizenship in my community implies. Issues of equity in community cease to apply, as diversity is an accepted feature of community. Diversity is clearly a norm in a community school and a desirable resource for the school. Individuals bring their particular characteristics, strengths and weakness to the table of community. Over time, we learn who we are in communities; we, also learn how each of us is different from others within our community.

A place where I belong is a place that knows me as an individual and not a bar coded number as part of the stock inventory that makes up a student body. Big schools tend to issue numbers for each of us, so that we can be sorted efficiently. Therefore, smaller schools are better for both students and teachers. In small schools, everyone knows my name and I know they know what I do and what I believe. Such schools are cherished by its members. Ted Sizer, writing in Meier (2000), continues the citizenship frame of reference, saying: "Perhaps also we need a fundamental redefinition of the obligations a growing adolescent must accept for himself and for the community of which he is a part, and then of what structures will help him reach of those obligations." (pp. 76-77) Deborah Meier (2000) herself quotes Joseph Priestly's remarks on the occasion of the dedication of New College, in London, in 1794: "...it is the great object of this institution to remove every bias the mind has been under, and to give the greatest scope for true freedom of thinking and equity (p. 81)."

There it is! A place where I belong is a community where every bias of the mind has been removed and where the curriculum invites, even challenges, its citizens to embrace "true freedom of thinking and equity." Creating such learning communities is not an easy task, but surely it is easier than giving into the domination of our hearts and minds by national agenda in education. The place to start is in our local communities where we can come to know who we are and what we dream of becoming. Furedi (2004) urges academics to overcome the fatalistic culture characterized by public passivity, and defend the importance of ideas and knowledge against today's philistines.

Issues and Questions for Chapter Eight

Living in a Complex World

- People want simple solutions, so they define their problems into simple ones, but what is attained by parsimony?
- The temptation of school politics is to construct either/or representations of reality.
- Anyone who has taught reading to beginning students knows reality is not a simple truth. (see: Booth, 2001) who tells us that...reading reality is a full contact sport."

Simple Curricula

- Teachers teach dinosaurs...Eskimos, penguins, year after year, in every grade from kindergarten to fifth grade. No wonder students get bored.
- Stotsky (1997) found that elementary teachers tend to focus on words of limited utility, so students do not have access to intellectual connectivity when reading new material. How many names for snow do the average students need to know?
- Langer (1997) describes meaningful learning as requiring multiple and different exposures to concepts.
- However, textbook guides tend to simplify the work for the teacher and in turn the teacher communicates vaguely about concepts rather than inviting engagement.
- Even at graduate school students tend to choose prescriptive definitions over descriptive observations,

so the constant look for formulas to capture experience, tends to dumb down reality, making it non-transferable. (See:Bateson, 2004).

Symptoms of Dumbing Down the Curricula

- Believing in myths about the real world rather than in the consequences of actions.
- Teaching for "skill attainment" locks students into contextually specific applications of learning.
- Focusing on accountability is buying someone else's definition of reality and how it should be understood.
- Textbooks tend to rob teachers of the exercise of their own intellectual engagement.
- Carving the school day into 45 minute time slots is a form of dumbing down the curriculum.

Overcoming the Achievement Gap Means Fighting Intentional Cruelty

- Educational Reform has not worked because it was intended to fail.
- Black/white issues dominate the "bottom line" accountability bandwagon.
- Schrag (2003) defines the improvement of education as an "adequacy issue"
- Minimalization in education parallels the minimaling movement in art.
- Examples of the Texas rules for achievement of standards...all rote learning examples.
- Class warfare is a key in understanding the Educational Standards Issues.American

Business Morality a Key to Understanding the Moral Intent of Dumbing Down the Curricula

- Executives in major corporations have divided the country into the haves and have nots; insisting that the "have nots" pay for the "haves" profits. While corporations pay no taxes, the burden for social support falls more and more on those with the fewest resources.
- Both urban and rural schools are capable of "blaming the victim." Conservative leadership in America urge universities to abandon "affirmative action" as undemocratic, but Edelman (1988) taught us to understand that the definers of problems are the ones who receive the "benefit" of the definitions.
- Hope for Revitalized Community
- Putnam (2002) writes about the revival of the sense of American Community.
- Schools cannot be isolated from their community context. So, the advocates of small and manageable schools have a major cause in their argument with the current "bigger is better" systems.
- Education is something that happens inside of people, not a program "run on" people.
- Creating a place where I belong is in fact creating community.

A FINAL NOTE

Since these chapters were written, Jonathan Kozol published his latest book, *The Shame of the Nation: The Restoration of Apartheid Schooling in America.* (NY. Crown, 2005). The book follows in the tradition of Kozol's criticism of our ineffective schools, in particular, this work offers documentation exposing the depth of the resegregation movement in American Schools. Kozol speaks for those disenfranchised students who go to schools that are under funded, under repaired, and under represented in the seats of administrative power brokers. Kozol's new book reminds us that instead of things getting better in American Education, they are actually getting worse. Over and over he documents the evidence that instead of improving equity in American Schools, the educational reform movements have actually exposed the poor to crushing burdens of isolation and oppression.

In the urban centers and in the south, schools systems have resegregated to such and extent that schools are more segregated at the beginning of the 21st Century than they were in the middle of the last century. Try this little experiment for yourself: look up the population identifications for various schools in America named in memory of Martin Luther King, Jr. in Los Angles (p. 24, 99% are black or Hispanic), or Rosa Parks School in San Diego (p. 24, 86% of the students are non-white, only 2% are classified as white), Thurgood Marshall in Seattle (95% are non-white, p. 22), and Langston Hughes in New York (p. 24, 99% are black or Hispanic). Given the research over the last 50 years that demonstrate that segregation reduces the chance of a superior education for students, these numbers are a telling documentation of our education failure. Or another statistic that is startling: in New York only 1 out of 7 black students in America go to a school that is predominately white. Black and other minority schools are: over crowded, in disrepair, have faculty less well prepared to teach reading, mathematics, and sciences, and are paid lower salaries than suburban schools. This is the story. In Kansas City, where the education reform movement focusing on desegregation began in the late 1950's, is today more concentrated, segregated and poorly run than they were 60 years ago with 99.6% of the students are non-white (p. 22). The grammar of segregation as separate education has proven the rule that it is not equal to mixed and unsegregated education, was applied by the nations courts with orders for busing students to provide some semblance of balanced populations in schools. By the late 1990s the courts turned around on the busing issue, under the pressure of the white suburbs and their real estate developers and one by one American cities returned to segregated schools under the rubric of "neighborhood schools."

One can find the most segregated schools by economic measures. The poorest communities are invariably segregated and isolated from the middle class students and their community schools. Now that the federal government has taken a hand in reform of education by "No Child..." measures, the numbers of segregated schools failing the tests standards is overwhelming. The federal government hides these facts by talk of making progress in improving our school. "No Child..." mandates are not making a difference in the bigotry and oppression visited upon the minority classes of our society. Offering rewards for success on passing averages to schools is really taking away from the poor and distributing to the rich. It is outrageous and insidious, but what is worse, so many educators seem to have bought into the formula for successes by testing. The Department of Education is providing support for 'scripted' reading and mathematics instruction. If teachers rebel, they are often transferred to another school. The rule is teach the content the feds' way or no way!

How does all this affect the disenfranchised student? Less than a third of minority students graduate from high school. Less than a third of those who do receive a high school diploma, are then accepted into higher education. Less than a third of those who go to college will finish with a college degree. Is this the success that the Department of Education claims for American Education? Is this creating a new and highly skilled corps of workers for our high tech economy? We think not and see the evidence in the outsourcing of American jobs overseas.

Jonathan Kozol is correct in describing American Education as the "Shame of the Nation." Only when the community rises up and takes control of the educational policies and curriculum for community students will American Education return to improving our schools and all that it means to the citizens of a democracy. No one is safe in a community controlled by others than the local citizenry. States' rights are essential to the success of educational opportunity for all. Communities must receive a fair share of the tax revenue in support of schools. No child should be unsupported in the quest for educational fairness and success. Those who pay the price, ultimately, are the marginalized students who are denied learning opportunities in favor of testing opportunities. In Michigan, high school students next year (2007) will spend 7.75 hours taking tests to demonstrate that they are proficient. And once again, the results are predictable; the marginalized students will fail in head to head competition with suburban white students. Kozol is right, it is a shame.

BIBLIOGRAPHY

Aguerrebere, J.A. (2003) *Charles W. Hunt Lecture.* 55th Annual Meeting of the American Association of Colleges for Teacher Education, New Orleans, LA. Unpublished Speech.

Altenbaugh, Richard J. (Ed.) (1992). *The teacher's voice: A social history of teaching in twentieth-century America.* London and Washington, D.C. The Falmer Press.

Alexander, P.A. (2000). "Toward a model of academic development: Schooling and the acquisition of knowledge." *Educational Researcher. AERA. 29.2 March, 2000. 28-33.*

Allington, R. (2000). *What Really Matters for Struggling Readers: Designing Research Based Programs.* Boston: Pearson Allyn & Bacon.

Apple, Michael. (1982). *Education and Power.* London: Routledge & Kegan Paul.

Apple, Michael. (1990). *Ideology and Curriculum.* NY and London: Routledge. 2nd. Ed.

Argyris, Chris. (1982). *Reasoning, learning, and action: Individual and Organizational.* San Francisco, CA: Jossey-Bass.

Argyris, Chris; Putnam, R.; and Smith, D.M.(1985). *Action*

Science: Concepts, methods, and skills for research and intervention. San Francisco, CA: Jossey-Bass.

Arrowsmith, William. (1971). The future of teaching. In Don Bigelow, Editor. *The Liberal arts and teacher education.* Lincoln, NB: University of Nebraska Press. (pp. 37-53).

Arsen, David and Plank, David N. (November, 2003). *Michigan School Finance Under Proposal A: State Control, Local Consequences.* The Educational Policy Center at Michigan State University.

Ayers, W. (2000). The Standards Fraud. In Deborah Meier, et al. *Will Standards Save Public Education?* Boston: The Beacon Press. 64-77.

Barth, Roland S. (1990). *Improving schools from within.* San Francisco, CA: Jossey-Bass.

Bass, Thomas A. (1994). *Reinventing the future: Conversations with the world's leading scientists.* Reading, MA: Addison-Wesley Publishing Company.

Bateson, Gregory. (1972). *Steps to an ecology of Mind.* New York. Ballantine Books

Bateson, Gregory. (1980). *Mind and nature.* London: Fontana Paperbacks.

Bateson, Mary Catherine. (2000). *Full Circles, Overlapping Lives: Culture and Generation in transition.* NY: Random House.

Bateson, Mary Catherine. (February 2004). Unpublished paper given at the American Association of Colleges of Teacher Education Conference.

Bell, L.A., Thomas, S., Shobo, A., Pizzolato, J. (Fall, 2004) "Special Issue on Accountability and Equity" American Education Research Journal. Vol. 41. No. 3. pp. 497-499.

Bellah, Robert N.; Madsen, Richard; Sullivan, William M.; Swidler, Ann; Tipton, Steven M. (1991). *The Good society.* New York: Alfred A. Knopf.

Bellah, Robert N.; Madsen, Richard; Sullivan, William M.; Swidler, Ann; Tipton, Steven M. (1985). *Habits of the heart.* Berkeley, CA: University of California Press.

Ben-Peretz, Miriam. (1990). *The teacher curriculum encounter: Freeing teachers from the tyranny of texts.* Albany, NY: State University of New York Press.

Berlin, Isaiah. (1991). *The Crooked Timber of Humanity: Chapters in the History of Ideas.* Ed. by Henry Hardy. New York: Alfred A. Knopf.

Berliner, D. & Biddle, B. (1995). *The manufactured crisis. Myths, Fraud, and the attack on America's Schools.* Reading, MA: Addison Wesley.

Bernstein, Richard J. (1992). *The New constellation: The ethical-political horizons of modernity/postmodernity.* Cambridge, MA: The MIT Press.

Berry, Wendell. (1990). *What are people for?* San Francisco: North Point Press.

Berry, Wendell. (1995). *Another turn of the crank.* Washington, DC. Counterpoint Books.

Berry, Wendell & David James Duncan. (2003). Citizens *Dissent: Security, Morality, and Leadership in an Age of Terror.* Great Barrington, MA: The Orion Society

Blau, Herbert. (1992). *To all appearances. Ideology and Performance.* New York: Routledge.

Bloom, H. (2000). *How to Read and Why.* NY: Scribner.

Booth, E. (2001). *The Everyday Work of Art: Awakening the Extraordinary in Your Daily Life.* Lincoln, NE : Authors Guild Backinprint Edition.

Brophy, J. and Good, T. (1986). Teacher behavior and student achievement. M.C. Wittrock (ed.), *Handbook of Research on Teaching.* Third Edition, 328-357. NY: MacMillan.

Boorstin, Daniel J. (1992). *The Creators: A History of Heroes of the Imagination.* New York: Random House.

Bowers, C.A. & Flinders, D.J. (1990). *Responsive teaching: An ecological approach to classroom patterns of language, culture, and thought.* New York: Teachers College Press.

Brook. Peter. (1995). *The Open Door: thoughts about acting and theatre.* London: Theatre Communications Group. Reprint Edition.

Bromwich, David. (1992). *Politics by other means: Higher education and group thinking.* New Haven, CN: Yale University Press.

Brown, M.K. et al. (2003). *Whitewashing Race: The Myth of a Color-Blind Society.* Berkeley, CA: University of California Press

Brown, Rexford G. (1991). *Schools of Thought: How the politics of literacy shape thinking in the classroom.* San Francisco, CA:Jossey-Bass Publishers.

Bruer, John T. (1993). *Schools for thought. A science of learning in the classroom.* Cambridge, MA: A Bradford Book. MIT Press.

Bruner, Jerome. (1990). *Acts of meaning.* Cambridge, MA: Harvard University Press.

Bruner, Jerome. (1996). *The Culture of Education.* Cambridge, MA. Harvard University Press.

Burke, J. (1999). *The Tao of Teaching, A Poetic Interpretation.* Paris, FR: Sophia Press.

Burke, J. and Johnston, M. (April, 2004). "Access to Higher Education." *Higher Education In Europe.* Vol. XXIX, No. 1. 19-31.

Burke, J. and Johnston, M. (Fall, 2004). "Students on the

Margins." *Journal of Race, Class, and Gender.* Vol. 11, No.3, 19-35.

Burke, J. and Johnston, M. (November, 2004). "Dumbing Down School Curricula." *Paper Presented at The International Conference on Social Science.* New Orleans, LA.

Camus, Albert. (1957/1963). Create Dangerously. *Resistance, Rebellion, and Death.* New York: The Modern Library.(pp. 208-209).

Changing Minds (Summer 1990) A publication of the Michigan Educational Extension Service. Helen Featherstone, Editor.

Cherryholmes, Cleo H. (1999). *Reading Pragmatism.* New York. Teachers College Press.
Chomsky, N. *(2003). For Reasons of State. NY: The New Press. Introduction by Arundhati Roy.*

Coggins, K., Williams, E. and Radin, N. (1997). The Traditional Tribal Values of Ojibwa Parents and the School Performance of their Children: an Exploratory Study. *Journal of Indian Education. 36 (3), 1-15.*

Cole, Stephen and Barber, Elinor. (2003). *Increasing Faculty Diversity: The Occupational Choices of High-Achieving Minority Students.* Boston, MA: Harvard University Press.

Coles, G., (2003). *Reading the naked truth: literacy, legislation and lies.* Portsmouth, NH: Heinemann.

Coles, Robert. (1989). *The call of stories: Teaching and the moral imagination.* Boston, MA: Houghton Mifflin.

Confrey, Jere. (1991). Steering a Course between Vygotsky and Piaget. *Educational Researcher.* 20 (8), 28-32.

Cone, J. (May/June, 2003). The construction of low achievement: A study of one detracked senior English class. *Harvard Education Letter.* 4-6.

Cortes, C. (2000). *The Children are watching: How the media teach about diversity.* New York: Multicultural Education Series. March, 2000.

Costa, A., Bena Kallick, & David Perkins, Eds. (2000). Activating & engaging habits of mind. (*Habits of Mind*, BK 2) ASCD ISBN 0871203693

Cuban, Larry. (1989). The persistence of reform in American schools. In Donald Warren (Ed.) *American Teachers: Histories of a profession at work.* NY: Macmillan. pp. 370-392.

Cunningham, P. & Allington, R. (2003). *Classrooms that Work. They Can All Read and Write.* Third Edition. Boston: Allyn & Bacon.

Csikszentmihalyi, Mihaly. (1990). *Flow: The psychology of optimal experience.* New York: Harper & Row, Publishers

Csikszentmihalyi, Mihaly & Eugene Rochberg-Halton. (1981). *The meaning of things: Domestic symbols and the self.* Cambridge: Cambridge University Press.

Cunningham, P. and Allington, R. (2000). *Classrooms that Work: They can all read and write.* Boston: Pearson Allyn & Bacon. 3rd Edition.

Damasio, A. (1994). *Descartes' Error: Emotion, Reason, and the Human Brain.* NY: G.P Putnam's Sons.

Damasio, Antonio. (2003). *Looking for Spinoza. Joy, Sorrow, and the Feeling Brain.* Orlando, FL: Harcourt, Inc. A Harvest Book.

Dance, L.J. (2002). *The Impact of Street Culture on Schooling.* New York: Routledge-Falmer.

Darling-Hammond, Linda, with Arthur Wise and Stephen P. Klein. (1995). *A License to teach. Building a profession for 21st Century Schools.* Bolder, CO. Westview Press.

Darling-Hammond, L., Jacqueline Ancess & Susanna Wichterle Ort.(2002) Reinventing high school: Outcomes of the coalition campus schools project. *American Educational Research Journal, 39,(3):639-673.*

Davies, Paul. (1992). *The Mind of God: Science and the search for ultimate meaning.* London: Penguin Books.

Dawkings, Richard. (1989). *The Selfish Gene.* Oxford: Oxford University Press. (New Edition).

Dean and Provost: Building and leading successful learning communities. "Community Colleges Dealing with Budget, Legal, and Transfer Woes." 5,3, p. 4.

Dehaene, S. (1997). *The Number Sense: How the Mind Creates Mathematics.* NY: Oxford University Press.

Dewey, J. (1898). *Lectures on Psychology and Political Ethics.* New York: Hafner Press, Reprint: (1976)

Dewey, John. (1944, reprint of original from1916). *Democracy in Education.* New York, Free Press.

Dews, C.L. Barney & Carolyn Leste Law. (1995). *This fine place so far from home: Voices of academics from the working class.* Philadelphia: PA Temple University Press.

Dill, David D. and Associates. (1990). *What teachers need to know: The knowledge, skills, and values essential to good teaching.* San Francisco, CA: Jossey-Bass.

Doll, William E. Jr. (1993). *A Post-Modern Perspective on Curriculum.* New York: Teachers College Press.

Dubner, S. (August 3, 2003). The Probability that a Real-Estate Agent is Cheating You (and other Riddles of Modern Life). *The New York Times Magazine.* 23-27.

Duderstadt, James. (May, 2004). Unpublished paper given at the Michigan American Council of Education Network Conference.

Dworkin, Dennis L. & Leslie G. Roman, Editors. (1993). *Views beyond the border country: Raymond Williams and Cultural Politics.* NY: Routledge. Critical Social Thought Series.
Eagleton, Terry. (2004). *After Theory.* New York: Basic Books.

Eco, Unberto. (1989) *The Open Work.* Translated by Anna Cancogni. Cambridge, MA: Harvard University Press.

Eco, Umberto. (1984) *Semiotics and the Philosophy of Language.* Bloomington, IN: Indiana University Press.

Edelman, Murray. (2001). *The Politics of Misinformation. Cambridge, UK.* Cambridge University Press.

Edelman, Murray. (1988). *Constructing the Political Spectacle.* Chicago: University of Chicago Press.

Edmundson, M. (2002). *Teacher: The One who made the Difference.* NY: Vintage Books.

Edmundson, M. (September 9, 2003). "How Teachers Can Stop Cheaters." *The New York Times.* Vol. CLII, No. 52,601. A31.

Egan, Kieran. (1983) *Education and psychology: Plato, Piaget, and scientific psychology.* New York: Teachers College Press.

Egan, Kieran. (1986). *Teaching as story telling: An alternative approach to teaching and curriculum in the elementary school.* Chicago, Illinois: The University of Chicago Press.

Englert, Carol Sue; Raphael, Taffy E.; Anderson, Linda M.; Anthony, Helene M.; Stevens, Dannelle. D. (1991). Making strategies and self-talk visible: Writing instruction in regular and special education classrooms. *American Educational Research Journal* <u>28</u> (2) 337-372.
Esquith, R. (2003). *There are no shortcuts* .NY: Pantheon Books.

Fenstermacher, Gary D. & Jonas F. Soltis. (1992). *Approaches to Teaching.* 2nd Ed. New York: Teachers College Press.

Ferris, Timothy. (1992). *The Mind's Sky: Human intelligence in a cosmic context*. New York: Bantam.

Ferguson, N. (April 13, 2003). "Overdoing Democracy" in *The New York Times Book Review*. Page 9. Review of Zakaria, F. (2003). *The Future of Freedom*. NY: Norton

Feynman, Richard. P. (1998). *The Meaning of it All. Thought of a citizen scientist*. Reading, MA. Addison-Wesley.

Foucault, Michael. (1989). *The Archaeology of knowledge*. London: Routledge.

Foucault, Michael. (1990). The History of Sexuality. Quoted by Murphy, W.T. in "Foucault: Rationality against Reason and History." *Reason and History or only history of reason?* Ed.by Philip Windsor. Ann Arbor, MI: University of Michigan Press.

Freedman, J. (2003). *Liberal Education and the Public Interest*. Iowa City: University of Iowa Press.

Furedi, Frank. (2004). *Where Have All the Intellectuals Gone? Confronting 21st Century Philistinism*. London & New York: Continuum International Publishing Group.

Gaines, D. (1998). *Teenage Wasteland: Suburbia's Dead End Kids*. Chicago, IL. University of Chicago Press.

Galeano, E. (1983). *Voices of Our Time*. San Jose, Costa Rica: EDCU

Gardner, H. (1983). *Frames of Mind: The Theory of Multiple Intelligences.* NY: Basic Books.

Gardner, H. (1989). *To Open Minds: Chinese Clues to the Dilemma of Contemporary Education.* NY: Basic Books.

Gardner, Howard, Mihaly Csikszentmihalyi & William Damon. (2001). *Good Work: When Excellence and Ethics Meet.* New York: Basic Books.

Geertz, Clifford. (1983). *Local knowledge.* New York: Basic Books.

Geertz, Clifford. (2000). *Available light. Anthropological reflections on philosophical topics.* Princeton, NJ. Princeton University Press.

Gibbs, Jeanne B. (1987). *Tribes: A process for social development and cooperative learning.* Santa Rosa, CA: Center Source Publications.

Giroux, Henry. (1988). *Teachers as intellectuals: Toward a critical pedagogy of learning.* New York: Bergin & Garvey.

Giroux, Henry. (1992). *Border crossings: Cultural workers and the politics of education.* New York: Routledge.

Gleick, J. (1988). *Chaos: Making a New Science.* NY Penguin Books.

Gleick, James. (1992). *Genius. Richard Feynman and modern physics.* London: Little Brown and Company.

Goodnough, Abbie. "High Stakes of fourth grade tests are driving off veteran teachers." *The New York Times,* June 14, 2001. A1 &A 29.

Goodman, P. (1962). *The Community of Scholars.* NY: Random House.

Gould. S. J., (2003). *The hedgehog, the fox, and the magister's pox. Mending the gap between science and the humanities.* NY: Harmony Books.

Graff, G. (2003). *Clueless in Academe: How Schooling Obscures the Life of the Mind.* New Haven, CN: Yale University Press.

Gratto, J. T., (2001). *A different kind of teacher. Solving the crisis of American schooling.* Berkeley, CA: Berkeley Hills Books

Gratto, J.T. (2002). *Dumbing us Down: the hidden curriculum of compulsory schooling.* NY: New Society Publishers, Paperback Second Edition.

Gratto, J.T. (2000). *The underground history of American Education: A school teacher's intimate investigation into the problem of modern schooling.* NY: The Oxford Village Press

Greene, Maxine. (1988). *The Dialectic of freedom.* New York: Teachers College Press.

Greene, Maxine. (1991). "Texts and Margins." *Harvard Educational Review*. Vol.61. No. 1; February, 1991. Reproduced in Merryl Ruth Goldberg & Ann Phillips, Editors, *Arts as Education.* Reprint Series No. 24. (1992). Cambridge, MA. Harvard Educational Review. 1-18.

Grudin, Robert. (1990). *The Grace of great things: Creativity and innovation.* New York: Ticknor & Fields.

Handal, Gunnar and Lauvas, Per. (1987). *Promoting Reflective Teaching: Supervision in Practice.* Milton Keynes, England: Open University Educational Enterprises, LTD.

Harris, Judith Rich. (1998). *The nurture assumption. Why children turn out the way they do. Parents matter less than you think and peers matter more.* New York. The Free Press.

Harris, Sam. (2004). *The End of Faith: Religion, Terror and the Future of Reason.* NY: W.W. Norton

Harrison, L. & Huntington, S. Editors. (2000). *Culture Matters. How Values Shape Human Progress.* NY: Basic Books.

Hawthorne, Rebecca Killen. (1992). *Curriculum in the making: Teacher choice and the classroom experience.* NY: Teachers College Press.

Heckman, J.J. and Krueger, A.B. (2003). *Inequality in America: What Role for Human Capital Policies?* Cambridge, MA: MIT Press.

Herbert, B. (2001, September 3). In America; On the way to nowhere.@ *The New York Times.* Page A15.

Herbert, B. (Friday, October 24, 2003). "Failing Teachers." *The New York Times.* A23.

Hobsbawm, Eric. (1992). "Introduction: Inventing traditions."

In Eric Hobsbawm and Terence Ranger (Eds.) *The Invention of Tradition*. Cambridge: Cambridge University Press, Canto Edition Paperbacks. pp. 1-14.

Hochschild, J. & Scovronick, N. (2003). *The American Dream and the Public Schools*. New York: Oxford University Press.

Hodgkinson, H. (2003). *Secondary Schools in a New Millennium: Demographic certainties, social realities*. National Association of Secondary School Principals (NASSP).

Holland, H. & Mazzoli, K. (2001). *The Heart of a High School: One Community's Effort to Transform Urban Education*. Portsmouth, NH: Heinemann.

hooks, bell. (1994). *Teaching to transgress*. NY: Routledge.

Howell, A. & Tuitt, F. Eds. (2003). *Race and Higher Education: Rethinking pedagogy in diverse college classrooms*. Harvard Educational Review Reprint Series No. 36. Cambridge, MA: Harvard Educational Publishing Group.
Huebner, D. (1997). "Poetry and Power: The Politics of Curriculum Development." in Finders, D. and Thornton, S. editors, *The Curriculum Studies Reader*. NY: Routledge.

Huxtable, Ada Louise. (Decemer 3,1992). Inventing American reality. *The New York Review of Books*. 39 No.20. 24-29.

Ignatieff, Michael. (1985). *The Needs of strangers*. New York: Viking Press.

llich, Ivan. (1973). *Tools for conviviality*. New York: Harper Colophon Books.

Jackson, Philip W. (1992). Conceptions of curriculum and curriculum specialists. In P. Jackson (Ed.). *Handbook of research on curriculum* (pp. 3-40). New York: Macmillan and A.E.R.A.

Jenkins, David (Bishop of Durham) & Rebecca Jenkins. (1991). *Free to Believe*. London: BBC Books (See Extract quoted in *The Guardian*, April 25, 1991, page 23)

Johnson, Mark. (1987). *The Body in the mind: The bodily basis of meaning, imagination, and reason.* Chicago: The University of Chicago Press.

Johnson, Mark. (1993). *Moral Imagination: Implications of cognitive science for ethics.* Chicago: The University of Chicago Press.

Jones, B., Valdez, G., Nowakowski, J., & Rasmussen, C. (1994). *Designing Learning and Technology for Educational Reform.* Oak Brook, IL: North Central Regional Educational Laboratory.
Kegan R. (1994). *In over our heads: The mental demands of modern life.* Cambridge, MA: Harvard University Press.

Kegan R. and Lakey, L. (2001). *How the way we talk can change the way we work.* San Francisco: Jossey/Bass.

Kennedy, D.M. (1999). *Freedom from Fear: The American people in depression and war, 1929-1945.* NY: Oxford University Press.

Kirp, D. (2003). *Shakespeare, Einstein, and the Bottom Line: The marketing of higher education.* Cambridge, MA: Harvard University Press.

Kliebard, Herbert M. *Forging the American Curriculum: Essays in Curriculum History and Theory.* New York: Routledge.

Kobrin, David. (1992). *In there with the kids: Teaching in today's classrooms.* Boston: Houghton Mifflin.

Kohn, Alfie. (1986). *No contest: The case against competition.* Boston, MA: Houghton Mifflin.

Kohn, Alfie. (1998). *What to look for in a classroom...and other essays.* San Francisco. Jossey-Bass

Kohn, A. (2000). *The case against standardized testing.* Portsmouth, NH: Heinemann.

Kolakowski, Leszek. (1990). *Modernity on endless trial.* Chicago: The University of Chicago Press.

Kotter, J. P., (1996) *Leading Change.* Boston, MA: Harvard School Press.

Kozol, Jonathan. (1991). *Savage inequalities: Children in America's schools.* New York: Crown Publishers, Inc.

Kozol, Jonathan., (2005). *The Shame of the Nation: The Restoration of Apartheid Schooling in America.* NY: Crown

Kripke, Saul A. (1982). *Wittgenstein on rules and private Language.* Cambridge, MA: Harvard University Press.

Kronholz, J. (August 20, 2003). "Flat College-Admissions

Scores Show Need for More Classwork." *The Wall Street Journal.*

Labaree, David F. (1997). *How to succeed in school without really trying. The credential race in American Education.* New Haven, CN. Yale University Press.

Labaree, D. (May, 2003). "The particular problems of preparing educational researchers." *Educational Researcher.* 32-4, 13-22

Langer, Susanne K. (1967). *Mind: An essay on human feeling.* Vol. I. Baltimore, MD: John Hopkins Press.

Lasch, Christopher. (1969). *The Agony of the American Left.* NY: Vintage.

Lather, Patti. (1991). *Getting Smart.* New York: Routledge, Chappman and Hall, Inc.

Lee, C. , Spencer, M., and Harpalani, V. (June/July, 2003) "Every Shut Eye Ain't Sleep": Studying How People Live Culturally. *Educational Researcher.* Vol. 32, No. 5, pp. 6-13.

Lentricchia, Frank and Thomas McLaughlin, Eds. (1990). *Critical Terms for Literary Study.* Chicago: University of Chicago Press.

Lemann, N. (2000). *The Big test: The secret history of American meritocracy.* NY: Farrar, Straus and Giroux.

Leonardo, Z. (April, 2003). The Agony of School Reform: Race, class, and the elusive search for social justice. *Educational Researcher.* Vol. 32, No. 3. AERA, 37-43.

Levine, A. & Cureton, J. (1998) *When Hope and Fear Collide*, San Francisco, Jossey-Bass.

Levine, Lawrence W. (1996). The Opening of the American Mind: Canons culture and history. Boston,MA: The Beacon Press.

Lieberman, Ann. Editor. (1988). *Building a professional culture in schools*. New York: Teachers College Press.

Lightman, Alan. (1992). "Inside the box." *New York Review of Books*. Vol. 39 No.44 February 13. pp. 37-38. Review of Timothy Ferris, *The Mind's Sky*. (1992).

Lincoln, Bruce. (1989). *Discourse and the construction of society: Comparative studies of myth, ritual, and classification.* NY: Oxford University Press.

Linn, R. (1998). *Standards –Led Assessment: Technical and Policy Issues in Measuring School and Student Progress.* National Center for Research on Evaluation, Standards, and Student Testing. CRESST Technical Report 490.

Little, Judith Warren & Milbrey Wallin BcLaughlin, Editors. (1993). *Teachers' Work: Individuals, colleagues, and contexts.* New York: Teachers College Press.

Lorenz, E. (1993). *The Essence of Chaos.* London: UCL Press.

Loury, Glenn C. (2002). *The Anatomy of Racial Inequality.* Cambridge, MA: Harvard University Press.

Lubrano, L. (2004). *Limbo: Blue-Collar Roots, White Collar Dreams.* Hoboken, NJ: John Wiley and Sons, Inc.

Macedo, D. (1994). *Literacies of Power: What Americans are not allowed to know.* Boulder, CO: Westview Press.

May, Rollo. (1991). The Cry for myth. New York: W.W. Norton & Co.

Macbeth, D. (Spring 2003, Vol. 40. No. 1). Hugh Mehan's *Learning Lessons* Reconsidered: On the differences between the Naturalistic and Critical Analysis of Classroom Discourse. *American Educational Research Journal.* pp. 239-280.

McCarthy, Thomas. (1991). *Ideals and illusions: On reconstruction and deconstruction in contemporary critical theory.* Cambridge, MA: The MIT Press.

McCourt, F. (1999). *>Tis, A Memoir .* N.Y. Scribner.

McDonald, Joseph P. (1992). *Teaching: Making sense of an uncertain craft.* NY: Teachers College Press.

McGilly, Kate. (Ed.) (1994). *Classroom lessons: Integrating cognitive theory and classroom practice.* Cambridge, MA: A Bradford Book. MIT Press.

McKeough, Anne & Judy L. Lupart, Editors. (1991). *Toward the practice of theory-based Instruction: current cognitive theories and their educational promise.* Hillsdale, NJ: Lawrence Erlbaum Associates.

McLaren, P. & Lankshear, C. eds. (1994). *Politics of Liberation: Paths from Freire*

NY: Routledge.

McLaren, P. (1989). *Life in Schools. An Introduction to Critical Pedagogy in the Foundations of Education.* NY: Longman.

McLaughlin, B. & McLeod, B. (1996). Educating All Our Students: Improving education for children from culturally and linguistically diverse backgrounds. Final Report of the *National Center for Research on Cultural Diversity and Second Language Learning.* Vol I. University of Santa Cruz, June, 1996.

McWhorter, J. (2000). *Losing the race: Self-sabotage in black America.* New York: Free Press.

McWhorter, J. (2003). *Authentically Black: Essays for the Black Silent Majority.* New York: Gotham Books.

Mathews, J. (September 30, 2003). "Class Struggle: A Coordinated Approach to Standardized Teaching." *The Washington Post.* Washington, D.C.

Medina J. and Lewin T. (August 1, 2003). High School Under Scrutiny for Giving Up on Its Students. *The New York Times.* Vol. CLII. #52,562, pages 1 and 16A.

Meier, Deborah. (1995). *The Power of their ideas. Lessons for America from a small school in Harlem.* Boston, MA. Beacon Press.

Meier, D. (2000). *Will standards save public education?* Boston: Beacon Press.

Meier, Deborah. (2002). *In Schools We Trust. Creating Communities of Learning in an Era of Testing and Standardization.* Boston, MA: Beacon Press.

Menand, Louis. (1992, June 25). *The real John Dewey.* [Review of *John Dewey and American Democracy by R.B. Westbrook}. The New York Review of Books.* 39 (12). 50-55.

Menand. Louis. (2001). *The Metphysical Club: A Story of ideas in America.* New York: Farrar Straus Giroux

Mitzman, Arthur. (2003). *Prometheus revisited: The quest for global justice in the 21st Century.* Amherst, MA: The University of Massachusetts Press.

Morgan, Wendy. (1997). *Critical literacy in the classroom. The art of the possible.* New York and London. Routledge.

Moses, R. & Cobb, Jr., C. (1999). *Radical Equations: Math Literacy and Civil Rights.* Boston: Beacon Press.

Mosley, Walter. (2000). *Workin'on the chain gang: Shaking off the dead hand of history.* New York: The Library of contemporary thought. The Ballantine Publishing Group.

Naipaul, V.S. (April 11, 1991). A handful of dust: Return to Guiana. *New York Review of Books.* 38. 7. 15-20.

Navarrette, R. (August 15, 2003). Teachers' Role in Learning Gap. *The Dallas Morning News, (Reprinted in the Sarasota Herald-Tribune, p. 13A).*

Newman, F., Secada, W. and Wehlage, G. (1995). *A Guide to Authentic Instruction and Assessment: Vision, standards, and scoring.* Madison, WI: Wisconsin Center for Education Research.

Nichols, P. (Winter, 1992). The curriculum of control: Twelve reasons for it: some arguments against it. *Beyond Behavior.* Vol. 3 No. 2.

Nieto, Sonia. (1992). *Affirming diversity: The sociopolitical context of multicultural education.* NY: Longman.

Noddings, Nel. (1984). *Caring: A femine approach to ethics & moral education.* Berkeley, CA: University of California Press.

Noddings, Nel. (1987). Fidelity in teaching, teacher education, and research for teaching. In Margo Okazawa-Ray, et al. eds. Teaching, teachers, and teacher eduation. Cambridge, MA: Harvard Educational Review. pp. 384-398.
Noddings, N. (1997). "Does Everybody Count?" in Finders, D. and Thornton, S. editors, *The Curriculum Studies Reader.* NY: Routledge.

Nozick, Robert. (1981). *Philosophical Explanations.* Cambridge, MA: Harvard University Press.

O'Connor, Alan. (1989). *Raymond Williams: Writing, culture, Politics.* Oxford: Blackwell.

Ohana, C. (2003). *Partnerships in Math Education. The power of university-school collaboration.* Portsmouth, NH: Heinemann.

Okazawa-Ray, Margo, James Anderson, and Rob Traver, Editors.

(1987). *Teaching, teachers, & teacher education.* Cambridge, MA: Harvard Educational Review.

Oliver, D. (1990, September). Grounded knowing: A postmoder perspective on teaching and learning. *Educational Leadership.* 48, 64-69.

Orfield, G. & Yun, J. (1999). *Resegregation in American Schools.* Cambridge, MA: Civil Rights Project. Harvard University.

Oser, Fritz K., Andreas Dick, Jean-Luc Patry, Editors. (1992). *Effective and responsible teaching: The new synthesis.* San Francisco: Jossey-Bass Publishers.

Paine, Lynn Webster, (1990). The Teacher as Virtuoso: A Chinese Model for Teaching. *Teachers College Record.* 921 Fall.

Palmer, Parker J. (1998). *The courage to teach. Exploring the inner landscape of a teacher's life.* San Francisco. Jossey-Bass Publishers.

Pelikan, Jaroslav. (1992). *The Idea of a University: A Reexamination.* New Haven,CN: Yale University Press.

Perry, William G. (1970). *Forms of Intellectual and Ethical Development in the College Years: A Scheme.* New York: Holt, Rinehart and Winston.

Phillips, D.C. & Soltis, J.F. (1991). *Perspectives on learning.* 2nd Edition. New York: Teachers College Press.

Piaget, Jean. (1976). *To understand is to invent: The future of*

Education. George-Anne Roberts, Translator. New York: Penguin Books.

Pinker, S. (2002). *The blank slate: The modern denial of human nature*. NY: Viking Press.

Popper, Karl. (1944/1985). "Piecemeal Social Engineering." *Popper Selections*. Ed. by David Miller. Princeton, NJ: Princeton University Press. pp. 304-318.

Portes, A. & Rumbaut, R., eds. (2001). *Legacies: The Story of Immigrant Second Generation*. Berkeley, CA: University of California Press.

Putnam, Hilary. (1990). <u>Realism with a human face</u>. Cambridge, MA: Harvard University Press.

Putnam, Hilary. (1988). *Representation and reality*. Cambridge, MA: The MIT Press.

Putnam, J., & Burke, J., (1992). *Organizing and managing classroom learning communities*. NY: McGraw-Hill.

Putnam, R. D. (2000). *Bowling Alone: The collapse and revival of American community*. New York: Simon & Schuster.

Putnam, Robert D. & Lewis M. Feldstein. (2003). *Better Together. Restoring the American Community*. New York: Simon & Schuster.

Raspberry, W. (October 13, 2003) " An Academic Achievement Gap." *The Washington Post.* p. A 19.

Ravitz, D. (2000). *Left Back: A century of failed school reforms.* New York: Simon and Schuster

Ravitch, D. (2003). *The Language Police: How pressure groups restrict what students learn.* NY: Alfred A Knopf.

Reyes, E. de los, & Gozemba, P. (2002). *Pockets of Hope. How students and teachers change the world.* Westport, CN: Bergin and Garvey.

Rhodes, F.H. (2001). *The Creation of the Future: The Role of the American University.* Ithaca, NY: Cornell University Press.

Rodriguez, R. (2002). *Brown: The last discovery of America.* NY: Viking Press.

Rorty, R. (1998). *Achieving our Country.* Cambridge, MA: Harvard U. Press.

Rudolph, J. (2 March 2002). From World War to Woods Hole: The use of wartime research models for curriculum reform. *Teachers College Record.* Vol. 104, No. 2. 212-241.

Sacks, P. (1999). *Standardized Minds. The high price of America's testing culture and what we can do to change it.* Cambridge, MA: Perseus Publishing.

Sagan, Carl and Ann Druyan. (1992). *Shadows of forgotten ancestors: a search for who we are.* York: Random House New.

Scheffler, Israel. (1985). *Of human potential: An essay in the philosophy of education.* Boston, MA: Routledge & Kegan Paul.

Scheffler, Israel. (1991). *In praise of the cognitive emotions and other essays in the philosophy of education.* NY: Routledge.

Schlosser, E. (2001). *Fast Food Nation: The Dark Side of the All American Meal.* NY. Houghton Mifflin.

Scholes, Robert. (1989). *Protocols of reading.* New Haven, CN: Yale University Press.

Scholfield, J.W. (1981). Complementary and conflicting identities: Images and interaction in an interracial school. In S.R. Asher & J.M. Cottman (Eds.), *The development of children's friendships.* (Pp. 53-90), Cambridge, UK: Cambridge University Press.

Schrag, Peter. (2003). *Final Test: The Battle for Adequacy in America's Schools.* New York: The New Press.

Schroeder, William. (1986). A teachable theory of interpretation. *In Cary Nelson (Ed.) Theory in the classroom.* Urbana, IL: University of Illinois Press. pp. 9-44.

Scribner, Sylvia. (November, 1984). *Literacy in three metaphors. American Journal of Education.* 6-20

Searle, John R. (1992). *The rediscover of the mind.* Cambridge, MA: The MIT Press.

Searle, John R. (1998). *Mind, language, and society. Philosophy is the real world.* New York. Basic Books.

Seligman, D. (1992). *A question of intelligence: The IQ debate in America.* New York: Birch Lane Press.

Selznick, Philip. (1992). *The moral commonwealth: Social theory and the promise of community.* Berkeley: University of California Press.

Sengupta, Somani. "How Many Poor Children is Too Much?" *The New York Times*, 7/8/01

Shannon. P. (1992). Becoming Political: Readings and Writings in the Politics of Literacy Education. Portsmouth, NH. Heinemann.

Shipler, D. (2004). *The working poor. Invisible in America.* New York: Alfred A. Knopf.

Shipps, Dorothy. (Winter 2003). "Pulling Together: Civic Capacity and Urban School Reform." *American Educational Research Journal. Vol. 40, No 4.* 841-878.

Shor, Ira. (1992). *Empowering Education: Critical teaching for social change.* Chicago: The University of Chicago Press.

Shulman, Lee S. (February, 1987). "Knowledge and teaching: Foundations of the new reform." *Harvard Educational Review.* Vol. 57, No.1 1-22.

Shulman, L. (July/August, 1999). Taking Learning Seriously. *ChangeMagazine*

Simon, Herbert A. (1991) *Models of my life*. New York: Basic Books.

Slavin, Robert.E. (1996). *Education for All. Contexts for learning.* Switzerland: Lisse. Swets & Zeitlinger. Publishers.

Smagorinsky, Peter and Michael W. Smith. (Fall, 1992). The nature of knowledge in Composition and literary understanding: The question of Specificity. *Review of Educational Research.* Vol. 62. No. 3 pp. 279-305.

Smith, D. (2002). *The Stone Flower Garden.* New York, NY: Warner Books.

Smith, F. (2003). *Unspeakable Acts, Unnatural Practices: Flaws and Fallacies in "Scientific" Reading Instruction.* Portsmouth, NH: Heinemann

Sternberg. R. (April,1998). Abilities are forms of developing expertise. *Educational Researcher.* 27/3. American Educational Research Association. 11-20.

Stotsky, Sandra (1997). "Why Today's Multicultural Basal Readers May Retard, Not Enhance Growth in Reading." *Readings on Language and Literacy: Essays in honor of Jeanne S. Chall.* L. R. Putnam, Editor. Cambridge, MA: Brookline Books. (259-286)

Strom, S. (2003). "Uproar in Kansas City over Foundation Chief." *The New York Times.* Monday, October 20, 2003, A8.

Taylor, Charles. (1989). *Sources of the self: The making of the modern identity*. Cambridge, MA: Harvard   University Press.

Taylor, Charles. (1992). *Multiculturalism and the politics of recognition: an essay with commentary*. Amy Gutmann, editor, et al. Princeton, NJ: Princeton University Press.

Taylor, Mark C. "What Derrida Really Meant." *The New York Times OP-ED*. October 14, 2004. Vol. CLIV ... No. 53,002.

Terkel, Studs. (1988). *The great divide: Second thoughts on the American dream*. New York: Pantheon Books.

Thernstrom, A. & Thernstrom, S. (2003). *No excuses: closing the racial gap in learning*. New York: Simon & Schuster

Thomason, T. (1999). *Improving the Recruitment and Retention of American Indian Students in Psychology*. Eric Number ED434790.

Toulman, S., Rieke, R., & Janik, A. (1984) *An introduction to reasoning*. New York: Macmillan.

Tyack, David and Larry Cuban. (1995). *Tinkering toward utopia. A century of public school reform*. Cambridge, MA. Harvard University Press.

Walker, Decker F. & Soltis, Jonas F. (1992) *Curriculum and Aims*. 2nd. Ed. New York: Teachers College Press.

Watkins, T. (2003). Public Statement at a Board of Education Meeting in Michigan, October 22, 2003

West, Cornel. (1999). "The Moral Obligation of living in a democratic society." In B. Batstone and E. Mendieta. *The Good Citizen*, NY Routledge, 1999, p. 12

Westbrook, Robert B. (1991). *John Dewey and American Democracy.* Ithaca, NY: Cornell University Press.

Westbrook, Robert B. (1996). "Public schooling and American Democracy." in Roger Soder, editor. *Democracy, education and the schools.* San Francisco. Jossey-Bass

Wilgoren, Jodi. "Education study finds U.S. falling short. Teachers are found not benefiting in era of economic Expansion." *The New York Times.* June 13, 2001. A28

Williams, L.F. (2003). *The Constraint of Race: legacies of white skin privilege.* University Park, PA: The Pennsylvania State University Press.

Winerip, M. (April 23, 2003). On Education: The lasting legacy of a promise of free education. *The New York Times.* Page A26.

Winter, G. (April 23, 2003) New ammunition for supporters of do-or-die exams. *The New York Times.* Page A26.

Wolff, R.P. (1969). *The Ideal of the University.* Boston: Beacon Press.

Young, Robert. (1990). *A Critical theory of education: Habermas and our children's future.* New York: Teachers College Press.

Zakaria, F. (2003). *The Future of Freedom. Illiberal democracy at home and abroad.*
NY: W.W. Norton & Company.

Zezima, K. (June 4, 2003). Hard Work Opens College Door for a Class. *The New York Times.* A29.